THE
AGE OF
PEACE

*Peace is the only culture for
both man and the universe*

MAULANA WAHIDUDDIN KHAN

CPS International USA

First published 2015
This book is copyright free

CPS International USA
2665 Byberry Road, Bensalem, PA 19020, USA
Tel. 617-960-7156
email: cps@alrisala.org, www.alrisala.org

IB Publisher Inc.
81 Bloomingdale Rd, Hicksville
NY 11801, USA
Tel. 516-933-1000
Toll Free: 1-888-560-3222
email: info@ibpublisher.com
www.ibpublisher.com

Goodword Books
A-21, Sector 4, Noida-201301, India
Tel. +91-8588822675, +91120-4314871
email: info@goodwordbooks.com
www.goodwordbooks.com

Printed in the United States of America

Contents

Foreword   5

Peace for the Sake of Peace

On Pacifism   10
Peace: the Summum Bonum   13
Peace and Justice   16
The Power of Peace   19

The Advent of the Age of Peace

The Age of De-monopolization   24
Western Civilization   27
The Age of Alternatives   30
The Age of Civilization   34
The Journey to Civilization   37
Making a Friend out of an Enemy   40

The Non-Confrontational Methods for Peace

The Creation Plan of the Creator   44
The Policy of Mutual Non-interference   47
The 'Save Yourself' Formula   50
The Policy of Delinking   53
The Power of Peace is Greater than the Power of Violence   56
The Examples Set by Two Prophets   59
An Institutionalized Buffer   62

The Experience of History

Living between Idealism and Pragmatism   66
Peaceful Planning on the Basis of Realities   69
Violent Activism, Peaceful Activism   73
A Prediction that Proved to be True   76
Unending War   79
The Problem of Crisis Management   82
Maintain the Historical Status Quo   85
Lessons from History   88

The Need for a Counter-Ideology

The Case of Present-Day Muslims 94
It Requires a Literary Bomb 97
Radicalization of Muslim Youths 101
The Evil of Selective Information 105
Suicide Bombing 109
It All Depends on the Angle of Vision 112
Living in a New Age 116
Why are the Youth Joining Terrorist Groups? 119
Peace through Education 122

Peace in the Muslim World

Peace of Mind is Most Important 126
The Unfinished Agenda 130
De Gaulleism Shows the Way 133
Low Profile, High Profile 136
The Road to Peace 139
The Crusades as Trendsetter 142
The Vatican as a Principle 145
Pro-Self Activism, Anti-Self Activism 149
The Culture of Terrorism 153
A Personal Experience 156

Islam and Peace

Islam the Religion of Peace 160
Interdependence—A Law of Nature 163
The Greatest Evil of History 166
God Calls to the Home of Peace 169
Managing Human History 172
Universal Peace Centre 175

Notes

Notes 178

Index

Index 184

Foreword

It was January 12, 2015. I was lying on a bed in New Delhi's Max Hospital, experiencing severe pain after surgery. The doctor eventually entered my room and said: 'Don't worry, this is a temporary phase. Soon everything will be normal.'

I had not slept the entire night and these words of the doctor set me thinking. I began to reflect upon those who were nowadays engaged in a self-styled holy war.

These perpetrators of violence have made other people their target everywhere—in places of worship, markets, hotels, public places, even graveyards. The violence unleashed by them has led to the merciless killing of large numbers of innocent people. I was then reminded of a verse from the Quran which tells us that killing one human being is akin to killing all of mankind. (5:32) There are now more than seven billion people in the world. This means that those who kill even a single person deserve the punishment of killing seven billion people. I was very distressed when this thought came to my mind and I questioned myself as to how those who killed others would bear such severe punishment.

What is the reason behind the seriousness of the issue of human killing? It is because this matter apparently pertains to human beings, but in reality it pertains directly to God. This means that killing a human being is tantamount to intervening in the creation plan of God. It is to deprive a person of the chance to live his full life and play the role destined for him by his Creator. It is only when a person lives out the full span of his life as granted to him by the Creator, that he is able to play the role assigned to him in this world.

Indeed, both killing and giving life pertain directly to God Almighty. Once a person understands the seriousness of this matter, he will never dare to kill anyone.

Thinking on these lines, I started to ponder over the case of those who committed suicide bombings. Suicide is held illegal in all religions and legal systems of the world. There is a tradition of the Prophet of Islam according to which one who committed suicide would have to face eternal Hell. I shuddered at this thought and tears began to flow from my eyes when I thought about how those who committed suicide would endure eternal pain in the world Hereafter, when I myself was not able to endure a temporary pain of a much lesser intensity?

A companion of the Prophet once narrated the following tradition:

'We were accompanying the Prophet in a war (*ghazwa*). Along with us was a person named Quzman who had already embraced the faith. During the war he suffered a serious injury. People began to praise him before the Prophet for the bravery he had exhibited in the war. But the Prophet said: *Innahu min ahl an-naar.* That is, "He is surely one of the people of Hell." The companions were taken aback by the Prophet's words, so he asked them to go and investigate the matter. It was then learnt that Quzman had indeed been severely injured during the war and when he could not bear the pain any more, he killed himself with his own weapon [Quzman's case was that of suicide]. When the Prophet was told about this, he uttered these words: "God is great and I bear witness that I am His messenger."'[1]

That was a dreadful night for me. I decided that very night that, after my recovery, the first task I would undertake would be to write a book on peace. The present book is the result of the decision I took while in bed in hospital.

The purpose of this book is to re-engineer the minds of those who think in terms of violence. The book aims at making such people realize that it is entirely possible for them to successfully achieve by peaceful means what they are unable to achieve by violent means.

May God accept the spirit of the writer in this regard and make this book a means of ushering in a new revolution which takes human history from violence to peace.

My gratitude is due in particular to two ladies who have greatly helped me in the preparation of this book—Dr. Farida Khanam, who is Professor at Jamia Millia Islamia, New Delhi and Maria Khan, who after doing her BSc in physics is now pursuing her doctorate in Islamic Studies at Jamia Hamdard, New Delhi. I would also like to thank Aijaz Ahmed who has read and commented on the manuscript. May God bless them all!

Wahiduddin Khan

New Delhi, July 26, 2015

Chapter One
Peace for the Sake of Peace

On Pacifism

⚜

*P*acifism is a doctrine subscribed to by all those who find war and all its attendant evils abhorrent—violence, destruction, loss of life and, in particular, the disruption of normal human existence. Throughout the ages, from the earliest times, peace has been a subject of compelling interest and study for all thinking people. Right from Aristotle to St. Augustine, from Bertrand Russell to Mahatma Gandhi, great minds have been preoccupied with this subject and have advocated adherence to the ways of peace. 1937 even saw the publication of an Encyclopaedia of Pacifism, yet a generally acceptable formula for establishing peace has yet to be arrived at.

The basic question is: peace for what? Or what is the criterion of peace? Pacifists generally maintain that peace must include social justice, or that peace is only that which gives justice to all. The Constitution of the International Labour Organization, a United Nations body dealing with labour issues, affirms,

> 'Universal and lasting peace can be established only if it is based upon social justice.'[1]

This concept of peace has won general acceptance among scholars.

The question arises as to how peace in this sense has never been established throughout human history, that is, peace with social justice. History itself provides empirical proof of the fact that this definition of peace is not in accordance with the law of nature. And it is a fact that, in this world, one cannot achieve anything without adhering to natural laws.

The reason behind this failure to establish peace is that almost all the scholars have bracketed peace along with certain irrelevant factors. Their concept of real peace is one in which there is no injustice, no violation of human rights, no inequality and no violence of any kind.

Let us take the analogy of the soil giving us the foodstuffs without which we cannot continue to exist. According to the law of nature, we have first to acquire fertile land and then prepare it for the cultivation of crops. The same is true of peace. Peace is like 'social soil', by cultivating which we can receive the fruits of social justice. Just as it is not possible to derive food directly from the soil, similarly we cannot derive social justice directly from peace.

According to the law of nature, peace can be attained only on a unilateral basis, and not on a bilateral basis. This means that first of all we have to abandon all kinds of confrontational methods such as political activism, protest-based activism and human rights activism. This kind of unilateralism will establish normalcy, normalcy will then lead to peace and peace will open the door to all kinds of opportunities. Then, by wise planning we can achieve all those goods that we want in terms of social justice and human rights.

According to the law of nature, peace can be attained only on a unilateral basis, and not on a bilateral basis.

This may be called a peace strategy. One historical example of this is the Hudaybiyyah Treaty entered into by the Prophet of Islam in 628 AD. This entailed the Prophet having to agree to all of the conditions demanded by his opponents. Such concessions may have seemed demeaning to his compatriots at the time, but the main feature of the treaty was that it guaranteed a lengthy period in which no war could be waged.

In essence, it amounted to a ten-year no-war pact, which gave the Prophet and his companions ample opportunities to spread the message of Islam far and wide.

This was a great success story and, by studying its implications, we can form a complete picture of the subject and develop a successful method for achieving the desired goal.

Peace can be established on a unilateral basis, without confrontation with others. But when we want to establish social justice and human rights, it becomes a bilateral issue, because we have to fight other groups which we think are responsible for injustice and the violation of human rights. If we start our journey towards this goal, it is bound to lead to confrontation with existing groups and, instead of reaching the desired goal, the concerned people will become engaged in violence. So we have to evolve a method that will work without involving confrontation with other established groups. Indeed, the achievement of social justice or human rights calls for very wise planning. It is not a journey along a highway, but through thickets of thorny bushes.

Therefore, peace for the sake of social justice is not a practicable formula. There is only one workable formula and that is peace for the sake of normalcy. Normalcy gives us the opportunity to do the wise planning necessary to achieve our goal.

Wise planning is non-controversial in nature. It is something that can be done without engaging in any kind of confrontation with others, regardless of the section of the society to which they belong. The formula in this regard is: Establish a peaceful atmosphere at any cost: it will open up all kinds of opportunities and then by availing of these opportunities through wise planning, we can achieve success.

Peace: the Summum Bonum

⟡

*L*iterally meaning the greatest good, *summum bonum* is an end in itself and at the same time contains all other goods. What, in practice, is the summum bonum? People have different opinions on this. Most people hold that freedom is the greatest good, but freedom cannot be so described. For the summum bonum is something the maximum use of which does not have any negative results, while the unchecked use of freedom can result in anarchy. Anarchy is something which creates unmanageable problems and which is bound to jeopardize the success of all kinds of developments, both material and spiritual.

The truth is that the true summum bonum is peace, which is good in all situations. Whatever use we make of peace, it never has any negative effects. Peace brings normalcy. That is the best thing about it, for all developments and progress can take place only in a normal situation.

There are two kinds of peace: individual peace and social peace. Another name for individual peace is peace of mind. Peace of mind is of the utmost importance for all individuals. Peace of mind is an issue of self-management and only if one is able to manage oneself, can one enjoy peace of mind. Bringing peace to society, on the other hand, is an issue of social management.

When we look at history, we find that social management, in the ideal sense, is an elusive goal. Those reformers who have worked for ideal social peace have seen their endeavours result in violence instead of leading to social peace.

What is the reason for this negative outcome? The reason is that these social activists have linked the concept of social peace with social justice. They have developed the theory that there is no social peace without social justice. First of all they felt they had to establish social justice, and then as a result social peace would ensue.

But this theory is quite unnatural, and therefore not workable. According to the law of nature, the role of peace is to provide the basis for all kinds of activities, by availing of which we can achieve the goal of justice. The basic role of peace is to establish normalcy, that being a prerequisite for all kinds of success. So, first of all we have to establish peace at any cost.

The problem is that social peace is a bilateral issue. There are always several groups which make up a society. It is a sine qua non that it is only when all the groups accept the scheme of peace, that there can actually be peace.

Then, what is the mutually acceptable position for every section of the society? The best formula for peace is status quoism. That is, if one tries to bring about change in the status quo, this can lead to violence, but if one accepts it, then there is peace.

The practicable formula in this situation can be expressed thus: Idealism with regard to individual peace and pragmatism with regard to social peace. In this scheme of things, no other formula will work.

After the Second World War, both Germany and Japan tried to re-develop their countries which had been devastated by war. For this purpose a peaceful environment was necessary in both the countries. But there were some problems. For example, Germany had lost the eastern part of its land. This was true also of Japan, which had lost its strategic island of Okinawa. But both adopted the formula of status quoism.

Without attempting to change the existing state of affairs, they began to execute their plan of re-constructing their countries by using the resources which were still within their control. Both proved to be successful and achieved a high standard of development within a short period of time.

> *Accept the status quo and try to achieve your goal by peaceful planning. In this way you will certainly achieve success.*

This is the only way to establish peace in society. If one wants to achieve any goal, spiritual or material, one has to follow this formula: Accept the status quo and try to achieve your goal by peaceful planning. In this way you will certainly achieve success.

It is a fact that peace is the summum bonum, but if you want to establish peace you shall have to follow the law of nature—that is, that peace provides the basis for performing all activities and is not the result of these activities. The right way is to first develop the correct basis and then achieve your goals through wise planning.

Peace is like the soil. Without the soil there can be no tree. Similarly, without peace there can be no social development.

Peace and Justice

❧

There are some groups in the modern world which are engaged in violence. If you ask them why they are spreading bloodshed, they will answer: 'We are victims of injustice. Give us justice and we will give you peace.'

This condition for peace is unnatural. It is impossible to achieve justice by fighting for it. This is like putting the cart before the horse. In this world, everything follows the law of nature and the task of achieving justice is no exception.

According to the law of nature, justice cannot be given to someone as a gift. The correct approach is first of all to establish peace on a unilateral basis. Peace will open the door to all kinds of opportunities. Then, availing of these opportunities through wise planning will help you to achieve justice. There is no example in history of anyone attaining justice by fighting.

Peace is not desirable for the sake of justice; peace is desirable for the sake of establishing normalcy. When there is normalcy, every opportunity is available. It is by availing of such opportunities that one can achieve justice.

Justice cannot be achieved as a right: rather one receives justice when one proves oneself deserving of it. If you are complaining against social injustice, then blaming others for it is not the right approach. You should try rather to identify your own shortcomings. Because, according to the law of nature what you call injustice is the result of your own lack of merit. That is why to achieve justice you have to accordingly prepare yourself. Injustice can be removed through education and hard labour, not by demand. The strategy of complaint and protest will not give you justice.

Our world is a world of competition. In this world one can achieve something only on the basis of merit, and not through complaints and demands. There have been a number of great reformers whose goal was to achieve social justice through demands. But they failed. The reason for this was that their starting point was not realistic.

There is only one starting point, and that is, to educate people and make them deserving of being given justice. Justice is for the meritorious: it does not come automatically. If you deserve justice, you will certainly find it. However, if you lack the required merit, you will surely be denied justice. Like other things, attaining justice is also based on the well-known formula of give and take. If you pay the necessary price, you will achieve justice, otherwise not.

Peace is not desirable for the sake of justice; peace is desirable for the sake of establishing normalcy.

The other obstacle to attaining justice is that people are obsessed with the concept of ideal justice. Because ideal justice is not achievable, what people get is, according to them, less than their requirement. Therefore, even after getting it, they think they have not achieved enough. The fact is that, in this world, a person can only have working justice, and not ideal justice. This is why even when people are in the category of the haves, they think that they are in the have-nots category. Thus, the solution to the problem is to allay people's feelings of unrest, rather than their sense of injustice.

There is a record in history of violence breaking out because people feel injustice has been done to them. But the reality is that they consider that whatever they get is less than what they demand. So, they continue to feel a sense of injustice, although they do have whatever justice it was possible for them to have.

The way to bring an end to violence is to remove people's sense of injustice instead of urging them to engage in a struggle to achieve justice. Working justice is possible in all situations, whereas ideal justice is not.

The Constitution of the International Labour Organization affirms,

'Universal and lasting peace can be established only if it is based upon social justice.'[1]

But this assumption is unrealistic. The truth is that peace can be established only by the acceptance of the status quo. The religious equivalent of status quo is *qanaa'at*, that is, contentment. Through peace, opportunities are opened up and it is by availing of these opportunities that justice can be achieved.

The Power of Peace

Scholars generally define peace as the absence of war. This is a negative definition. The positive definition would be that it is a state in which there are a great many opportunities. The most important role of peace is that it opens up the door of opportunities, giving each and every individual the chance to avail of these opportunities and reach his or her goal.

Opportunities are most important in life. Success can be achieved when one recognizes these opportunities and avails of them with wise planning. It is therefore most important to establish peace in life, at any cost. Peace will open up opportunities and by availing of these opportunities one can achieve anything that one wants to achieve. Those who engage in violence demonstrate their unawareness of this law of nature.

For example, if those engaged in violence are asked the reason for their actions and whether they are not interested in peace, the response expected from them will be that they know that peace is good, but that they have been deprived of justice.

This answer is like putting the cart before the horse. The fact is that no one can give you justice as a gift. Justice is the result of one's own effort. First of all, you have to establish peace at any cost. Then, you have to commence your journey towards justice with wise planning. This is the only road to justice. No other road leads to this goal.

After the Second World War, the Allied Powers divided Germany roughly into two – East and West Germany. This strategy was designed to weaken Germany on a permanent basis. This was a clear case of injustice, but the German leaders did not react. What happened was that nature was given a chance to work. A peaceful process followed and nature silently worked to establish normalcy. The Berlin Wall eventually came down, and after forty-five years, Germany became united in 1990. Today both parts of Germany constitute a single country, just as it existed before the Second World War. West Germany never fought wars to annex East Germany. All the Germans did was to tread the path of peace.

Through violence you can cut down a tree, but violence cannot help you to grow a tree.

The greatest strength of peace is that it allows nature to work. If you want to achieve your goal through war, then you yourself shall have to fight. Peace on the other hand works on its own. If you stop war, peace will prevail. In this case, we only need to give nature a chance. In such a situation, nature starts to have an instant effect. The only condition is that when nature is at work, one must not interfere. Peace works only in an environment of non-interference. When there is interference, this process of nature comes to a halt. Just as after the seed is sown, the tree starts to grow on its own, this is also the greatest strength of peace. Those who understand this inherent power of peace are never confronted by failure.

Through violence you can cut down a tree, but violence cannot help you to grow a tree. This is true likewise of human life. In the human world, war only leads to destruction. Peace, however, has a positive role. No constructive work can be done if there is violence, whereas peace facilitates constructive work on its own. Peace paves the way for nation building along healthy lines.

War starts with anger and ends in anger. War does not have any healthy or constructive aspect, neither at the beginning nor at the end. But peace, from A to Z, is a healthy state of affairs. Peace, in every way, leads to a positive result, for it is in keeping with the law of nature. That is why, when a person adopts the peaceful method, the entire world of nature comes to his support. On the other hand, if a person adopts the violent method, the entire world of nature stands out in opposition to him.

Chapter Two

The Advent of
the Age of Peace

The Age of De-monopolization

God Almighty created man and settled him on the planet earth. He gave man total freedom, which he was required to use in a self-disciplined manner. But he failed to do so. Greed for political power, economic self-interest and religious intolerance became the order of the day. The situation continued for several thousands of years. This was the basic reason for the prevalence of the war culture in previous centuries.

This state of affairs was against the creation plan of God. According to the creation plan, it was required that every man and woman should have a free environment in which to develop his or her personality. But over time this scheme was vitiated. Then, God endeavoured to manage history while maintaining human freedom. This required very intricate planning. It therefore took a long time for the goal to be reached. The present age is the culmination of this divine planning.

The limited options available in earlier times gave way to the gaining of monopolies over all things: political power, economic opportunities and religion. Everything was monopolized by one group or another. In such a situation, the Creator wanted to de-monopolize all the resources of life so that every man and woman might have freedom of choice. Therefore, God initiated a process of management of history. Our modern civilization is the culmination of this long process of divine management.

The age of democracy brought the de-monopolization of political power. Modern industrialization was the outcome of de-monopolization in terms of economic opportunities. The modern age of intellectual freedom made possible the de-monopolization of religious dogmatism. The emergence of modern science led to the de-monopolization of ideological regimentation.

It is this phenomenon that the British writer J.F. West has rightly called a great intellectual revolution.[1] The de-centralization of all kinds of monopolies was bound to lead to a culture of peace. After de-monopolization, everything has come within everyone's reach, so that there is no question of having to indulge in violence to gain one's ends.

In previous ages, the choices were apparently very limited. It was this state of affairs that produced the culture of monopoly. Human beings were then divided into two groups: the haves and the have-nots. This division of people was bound to create a clash of interests between different groups. This was the main reason why people of the previous ages were frequently engaged in war and violence.

The de-monopolization of resources in the modern age is a great blessing, as it has made the violent method totally irrelevant. Now by peaceful methods, everything can be attained on a much greater scale

Modern civilization has virtually de-centralized all the opportunities of life. It has become possible for everyone to be free to achieve what he or she wants to achieve in the field of his or her choice. Then, why do we see that, even after the emergence of our modern civilization, the war culture has persisted in some quarters? The reason is unawareness of this change in history.

For example, if an individual wants to have political power, he does not need to wage war. In ancient times, a change in government could be brought about only by fighting and unseating the ruler from his throne. However, in a democracy, it is possible to take the place of the ruling party by the peaceful process of holding elections. It is these developments that have made the present age an age of peace, but to avail of the opportunities of this age requires education. This is why we see that in educated societies, a change in government is brought about smoothly by the peaceful process of holding elections, while in less educated societies, people, still in the grip of an outdated mindset, are still fighting to wrest control of political power.

The same is true of economic opportunities. Our ancient economy used to be based on agriculture and only by usurping others' lands could one increase one's production. Today, the vast field of industry has opened up and one can be successful by availing of the numerous opportunities offered in this sphere.

The de-monopolization of resources in the modern age is a great blessing, as it has made the violent method totally irrelevant. Now by peaceful methods, everything can be attained on a much greater scale. The end of the age of monopolization and the coming of the age of de-monopolization is, in other words, the end of the age of violence and the advent of the age of peace.

The age of de-monopolization has practically eliminated the option of war. Now opting for war does not arise out of any kind of necessity, but is only the result of the ignorant misuse of freedom.

Western Civilization

⟡

There are several verses in the Quran which make predictions of future events. For instance, the prediction of the victory of the Romans over Sassanid Persia (The Romans, 30:1–2). This prediction was fulfilled within ten years, as mentioned in the Quran. But of greater significance is the prediction in the Quran which clearly applies to the rise of western civilization – a pro-human civilization – in the later period of human history:

> 'We shall show them Our signs in the universe and within themselves, until it becomes clear to them that this is the Truth.' (41:53)

This verse clearly foretells the developments which took place in western nations one thousand years after the revelation of the Quran. This civilization of the West was, in reality, based on science. There are two aspects to this: the theoretical and the practical, or applied aspect.

The applied aspect of western civilization may also be called the technological aspect. It is this aspect which is mentioned in the following tradition of the Prophet:

> 'God will certainly support His religion with the *fajir* or non-believer.'[1]

Fajir here means a secular person. This saying of the Prophet is, in fact, a prediction of the emergence of western civilization which, in essence, was pro-human. That is, it would benefit all of mankind as well as the divine religion.

Western or modern civilization is not the property of a certain race or community. It owes entirely to the discovery of hidden natural laws and the development of a technology which benefitted and still benefits the entire humanity. For example, the discovery of the laws of nature introduced a new age of communication, from which everyone benefitted, including the proponents of the religion of Islam.

The evolution of western civilization has two sides to it. One pertains to the intellectual revolution brought about in the social and political world. For instance, one major step forward was the replacement of monarchy by democracy. The other side pertains to the benefits introduced by modern means of communication. This has given people a thorough knowledge of geography, and facilitated travel from one place to another. The printing press too has greatly facilitated the dissemination of ideas across the whole world. Electronic technology has, indeed, turned the whole world into a global village. Now it has become possible to speak from one part of the globe and be heard and watched across the world.

Western or modern civilization is not the property of a certain race or community. It owes entirely to the discovery of hidden natural laws and the development of a technology which benefitted and still benefits the entire humanity.

The greatest benefit of these modern developments is that for the first time in human history the age of peace has been ushered in. In earlier periods of human history, bloody battles had to be fought if any end was to be achieved. Everything was decided upon on the battlefield and because of this, a great number of human beings left this world without having performed their due role. In the wake of modern developments, for the first time in human history, it has become possible to achieve any target, great or small, through completely peaceful means.

Through long planning the Creator had brought about a revolution in human history, which brought the age of war to an end. In this way, it had become possible by using peaceful means to attain all ends in a way which was far better than the violent one which achieved nothing of any value.

This is the greatest achievement of the modern age. Those who adopt the method of war and violence in today's age only demonstrate that they are totally unaware of the modern developments of history. This crass ignorance is reflected in their reckless use of arms. By stooping to violence, they have committed the most heinous crime in history.

In such a situation, those who in the twenty-first century have abandoned the peaceful method and opted for the strategy of guns and bombs, are only proving that all they can carve out for themselves and others is a history of death and destruction, and in the Hereafter this verse of the Quran will apply to them:

'Those of you who act thus shall be rewarded with disgrace in this world and with a severe punishment on the Day of Resurrection.' (2:85)

The Age of Alternatives

⟡

*I*n ancient times, ambitious people had only one arena in which to fulfil their ambitions—the battlefield. But the modern age has seen a sea-change in this regard. Now we are living in the age of alternatives. There are many options other than engaging in battle.

For an ambitious person, a number of peaceful alternatives are available. Those gains that people expected only from war are now achievable, on a far greater scale, by availing of peaceful alternatives. To illustrate these points, I would like to give here two parallel examples.

The Mughal rule in India was a dynastic one. Aurangzeb (1618 – 1707) was the sixth ruler of this dynasty. He and his brother Dara Shikoh (1615 – 1659) had different agendas. At that time there was only one course available to settle the differences—that was battle. Therefore, a battle took place in which Dara Shikoh and his supporters were defeated and killed.

In present times, there are two major political parties in the same India—Congress and the BJP. These two parties have different agendas. Since India is now a democratic country, both parties contest elections to decide their fate, and this principle works. Thus, in May 2014 in the wake of the general elections, the political leadership of India changed peacefully.

This alternative is available in every country, even in those countries in which some groups are engaged in violence. Every day we hear news of bloodshed in these countries.

This state of affairs is due to our leaders' unawareness of how the times have changed. Those leaders who are engaged in violence in these countries are acting under the influence of an old mindset. According to this mindset, they are familiar only with the ancient model of kingship. They are unaware of the present democratic model. Although the result of this kind of violent struggle is very terrible, the conditioning of the way of thinking of these leaders is so deep-rooted that they are unable to rethink their strategy. In recent times, several leaders have become victims of violence, for example, Saddam Hussein (d. 2006), Abu Bakr al-Baghdadi (d. 2014, unconfirmed), and Abu Ala al-Afri (d. 2015).

The coming of the age of alternatives is a very positive sign. It means that history is moving from war to peace. In the twenty-first century this age has reached its culmination. Now there is no need to opt for the gun or the bomb culture. Any person who wants to fulfil his ambitions must take cognizance of the spirit of the age. Before taking any action, he must ponder over the whole situation. If he possesses an objective mind, he will certainly come to grips with the fact that he has a better option in terms of the peaceful method.

The coming of the age of alternatives is a very positive sign. It means that history is moving from war to peace.

One such example is modern Turkey. Towards the end of the nineteenth century, Turkey was part of the Ottoman Empire, which comprised about thirty present-day countries. But during the First World War, the Ottoman empire disintegrated and Turkey's political expansion was brought to an end.

However, in the wake of the dissolution of their empire, the leaders of modern Turkey took some drastic measures and searched for an alternative to political expansion—that is, the development of science and technology in their country. As a result of this, within a short period, Turkey emerged as the most developed country of the Muslim world.

Present-day Muslims are living in a political dichotomy, that is, in a condition in which there is the ruler and the ruled. They have found themselves reduced to the ruled category, which they find unacceptable. So they are trying to change this state of affairs and to bring themselves back into the ruler category.

But this dichotomous thinking is totally unrealistic. They are unaware of the fact that there exists a third option for them, of which they should avail. It is an option which is so great that, by exercising it, they can build a non-political empire for themselves.

The real problem is that present-day Muslims are ignorant of the fact that the present age is one of democracy. In this age, the government has been reduced to performing the role of administration. But, outside the administration, there are much bigger fields open to Muslims. For example, education, the press, the media, economics as well as *dawah* work, or conveying the message of God to people. Muslims would do well to abandon their political activism and dedicate themselves to the above non-political fields. Here, they can build independent universal empires, much greater than their former political empires.

It is a fact that in the present age there has been an alternatives' explosion in every field. Be it man or woman, skilled or unskilled, political leaders or reformers: this principle successfully applies to everyone. Now there is no need for pessimism or to engage in protests or violence or fighting, because everyone can easily come to know that there is an alternative for him or her and by availing of it, he or she can achieve success in any walk of life.

In the present age, the phrase 'armed struggle' may still appear in the dictionary, but it has no real meaning any more. Like other obsolete words, 'armed struggle' has also become obsolete. It is now a kind of anachronism to speak in terms of war and violence.

'Fighting' in the present world is an outdated concept. If the present fighters and militants were to become aware of this fact, they would surely throw away their weapons. Their weapons would only find a place in museums.

The Age of Civilization

⟶⟜

*V*iolence is a remnant of the culture of primitive society. In the early ages people knew only one way of settling their affairs—that of violence. It is said that at some point in the Stone Age two people, having started a quarrel, threw stones at each other in anger. The stones collided and this resulted in sparking. The two men observed the sparks that originated from the collision. They forgot their quarrel and began to ponder over the phenomenon of sparking. From this experience they discovered that there was something hidden in stones, which was separate from the stones. That is, the stones do not have light, but what resulted from their collision was light; stones are hard, while the spark was "soft", and so on. It is said that it was such events that started the pursuit of the study of natural laws.

It took thousands and thousands of years for man to discover that there are laws hidden in nature and that by understanding them we may harness the potential of nature for our benefit. The discovery of steam power is an example of this unfolding of the hidden potential of nature. Similarly, cars and aeroplanes were built by utilizing natural resources.

In this way, after a long period it became possible to convert matter into technology. This process went on uninterruptedly with a large section of humanity involved in it. A long time elapsed between the invention of the wheel and the development of modern means of communications. The results of the many discoveries and inventions during this period contributed enormously to modern civilization and completely changed human lifestyle.

The greatest characteristic of the civilized world is that it has enabled man to come out of the age of hardships and lead a comfortable life. Modern cities provide the amenities and environment which make this kind of life possible.

Modern civilization has, from every aspect, given a comfortable life to people—comfortable travel, convenient communication, well-equipped institutions. In short, all the activities of life have been made comfortable and convenient.

The developments of modern civilization have facilitated all the activities of modern living. Whether a person is at home, in his office or travelling, he enjoys a comfortable life. Today a civilized life means a comfortable life.

It took thousands and thousands of years for man to discover that there are laws hidden in nature and that by understanding them we may harness the potential of nature for our benefit.

The age of civilization has potentially brought the age of war to an end. War and violence in this age have become as irrelevant as trying to light a fire in the kitchen by knocking two stones together instead of using matchsticks or a lighter.

Nowadays, no one lights a fire in the kitchen in a way that has become obsolete. But we see that, even today, the way of war and violence is regularly opted for, although it is a completely uncivilized option—one which had relevance only in primitive ages.

Then why is it that, even in this age of civilization, the course of war is taken, and has not been entirely abandoned? The reason is that although man successfully discovered the method of converting matter into technology, he failed to discover the art of difference management. The art of difference management is still an underdeveloped science.

Difference is a part of nature. Difference serves as a boosting factor for one's intellectual development. If there are no differences, there will be no intellectual development. Therefore, difference is not an evil. The real problem arises when we are unable to manage differences.

What is the art of difference management? It is to settle differences through peaceful negotiations. It is to apply reason to the issue of differences such as was applied to the discoveries of nature.

Difference was always a part of human life. In primitive ages people tried to settle it through confrontation and fighting—this was a barbaric way. The civilized way of managing differences is to apply reason whenever there is an instance of difference and to try to settle it through peaceful dialogue.

The age of civilization is still incomplete. So far, it has only offered us material comforts. There is something yet to be achieved, and that is to peacefully settle differences in a civilized manner. On the day when people learn how to settle differences peacefully, the age of civilization will have reached its culmination.

The Journey to Civilization

*V*iolence erupts when anger goes unchecked. In life people have undesirable experiences on an almost daily basis: this is an integral part of our lives and it is what builds up a kind of suppressed anger in most human beings. Then, when some provocative situation arises, that latent anger flares up leading to violence and at times to war. A permanent solution to this scourge would be to find an effective method of stemming this flood of anger.

The best way would be to keep in mind the historic contribution of humanity at large. This realization would serve as an intrinsic check to violence.

At present, we are living in a civilized world; we enjoy numerous kinds of comforts and facilities. But these amenities were not available in the early history of humankind. How did they come into existence? It is the end result of a long process of development. Primitive man lived a life of hardship. Historians call this period the Stone Age. In this age everything was in its crude state. Then, man embarked on a long journey of development. First he travelled on horseback, then he invented the wheel and finally, by dint of long research, he developed technology, which consequently gave rise to travel by car and aeroplane. Humans in this way moved on from essentially crude means of securing comfort to modern technology. It was a long journey – the journey of civilization, in which all of mankind was, directly or indirectly, involved. People made great sacrifices, generation after generation. They spent their energy and time on developing things which would be of use to everyone. In this way, people planted a garden of civilization, the fruit of which we are now reaping. We thus owe a debt to the whole of humanity.

This is the true basis of universal fraternity. 'Love your neighbour' is a good formula. But, there has to be a rational basis upon which this principle is followed in actual life. Man is a justification-seeking animal. He requires a rationale for every action, even including that of having love and compassion for others. It is the above concept of the evolution of civilization that provides a strong basis for such a way of thinking.

A person would always try to avoid fighting against his parents, because he knows the contribution his parents have made to his life. People are aware of the contribution made by their parents, but they are unaware of the contribution of the greater humanity.

If they were to become aware of the contribution of humanity, they would love humanity more than they loved their parents, and would never take humanity as their rival. It is the sense of rivalry with others that leads to violence. If this rivalry ceased to exist, then violence would never be resorted to.

If people were to become aware of the contribution of humanity, they would love humanity more than they loved their parents, and would never take humanity as their rival.

Since man is a justification-seeking animal, without justification he does not do anything. If people were aware of the historical contribution of humanity to their lives, it would serve as a justification and they would never engage in rivalry with others. Instead, they would follow the principle of 'love all'. This is what provides the real intellectual basis for social peace.

All those consumer goods that we obtain from shopping centres today, all those facilities that make our life comfortable at home and outside the home when travelling have not been made by the present consumers. They have been developed by humanity over a long period of time. We use them without giving any thought to their origins. If we took all these things as gifts to us from humanity, we would regard others as benefactors rather than as rivals. All our negative thoughts for others would then be eliminated. We would live with the thrilling spirit of compassion for others. Thinking in this way would certainly root out the negativism that develops the 'we and they' concept, and sometimes flares up into violence.

A person who looks at things in this way will realize that the whole of humanity has a role to play in his existence. Till now he has been labouring under the illusion that, in his life, only his family has made a contribution, but now he will understand that humanity has played a much greater part in his life. He will come to think that without the contribution of humanity, he is nothing.

Each individual has strong affection for every member of his family. But if he develops the above universal thinking, he will feel strong affection for the whole of humanity. He will discover that Christ's saying 'Love your enemy' means 'Love all because all are your benefactors, there is no enemy.'

Making a Friend out of an Enemy

During a visit to the US in June 2011, I was invited to an American church in Philadelphia to deliver a lecture on the importance of peace. When I had completed my address, a Christian scholar asked: 'There is a well-known teaching in the Bible, "Love your enemy."[1] Can you refer to any such verse from the Quran?' I said, 'Yes, you can read verse 34 of Chapter 41 of the Quran. The translation of this verse is:

> "Good and evil deeds are not equal. Do good deeds in return for bad deeds; then you will see that one who was once your enemy has become your dearest friend."' (41:34)

This Quranic verse is based on the law of nature. According to the law of nature, there is neither a permanent friend nor a permanent enemy. People fall into two categories: some who are actual friends, and others who are potential friends. One must discover this fact and by right planning, try to turn this potential into actuality.

Those who are engaged in violence in the name of jihad tend to take things at face value. That is, if someone appears to be an enemy, they instantly declare him an enemy and initiate a bloody war against him. This is an example of their failing to go below the surface of things. However, if they looked at things in a deeper way, they would find that those whom they regarded as their enemies had, in reality, the potential of being their best friends. Therefore, instead of waging war against them, they should have made them their friends through peaceful *dawah* work, that is, by conveying the message of God.

According to the law of nature all men and women are children of Adam and Eve. That is, all human beings have a common ancestor. This means that mankind is a global family. All men and women are blood sisters and blood brothers. In the present day, this biological phenomenon has become a scientifically established fact. Now, it is no longer a mysterious story of Adam and Eve. Rather, it is a fact affirmed by anthropological research.[2]

The acceptance of this biological fact makes it possible, at least in terms of theory, for all men and women to live as a global family, rather than as rival groups. Now there is virtually no justification for tribal or national or any other kind of war in human society.

We seldom hear of fighting having broken out between members of the same family. Theoretically, this ought to be true for the whole of mankind, for, according to scientific research, all of mankind is a single family, and so, the old kinds of hostilities should come to an end. The time has now come for all of mankind to live on earth in harmony as a single family. Living in harmony is no longer simply an ethical principle. Rather, it is a way of life, the veracity of which has been proved through scientific studies.

In the present age, the scientific community has abandoned several ancient theories. For example, the heliocentric theory has replaced the old geocentric theory. The same approach is applicable to war and peace. The demands of a realistic assessment of current affairs and scientific thinking should make people give up violence and adopt the peaceful method as their only possible course of action.

The fact of common ancestry has forever done away with the equation of 'we and they'. Now the only valid equation is one that is based on the concept of 'we and we'. To initiate war, therefore, is like waging war against one's own family members rather than against any outside group. War is now the act of a pre-civilized age and not of modern civilization.

This universal fact is set forth thus in the Quran:

'...whoever killed a human being—except as a punishment for murder or for spreading corruption in the land—shall be regarded as having killed all mankind, and that whoever saved a human life shall be regarded as having saved all mankind.' (5:32)

War has only one serious upshot: the killing of others. War is, in effect, an act of mass murder. In this sense war is the worst kind of heinous crime. In other words, war means the killing of humanity and peace means the giving of life to humanity.

Killing a human being is not like killing an animal. Killing a member of humanity is like killing one's own self.

It is clear from the foregoing arguments that the sole option we have before us is not war, but peace.

Killing a human being is not like killing an animal. Killing a member of humanity is like killing one's own self. If one is aware of this reality, one will never make another human being the victim of one's violent actions. When one person kills another, it is out of ignorance. If people's lack of awareness in this regard could be remedied, then certainly violence could be brought to an end. The best way then to counter violence and war is to promote universal education.

Chapter Three

The Non-Confrontational Methods for Peace

The Creation Plan of the Creator

❧

We are not the designers of this world. This world was designed by a Mind far superior to ours. Therefore, we must follow the scheme of things as conceived of in the mind of the Designer. Our plans will otherwise result in failure.

Peace is one of the principles according to which the world has been designed. By following the peaceful method, there is nothing that we cannot achieve, while by ignoring the peaceful method all our planning will result in total failure. This is a reality expressed thus by the Prophet of Islam:

'God grants to peace what He does not grant to violence.'[1]

This prophetic tradition is a statement of a law of nature. This law of nature is in no way mysterious: every person can understand it just by reflecting on nature. The law of nature is that in this world only a peaceful plan can work. A violent plan cannot work at all.

The rationale behind this natural principle is that when one opts for the peaceful method, one is choosing to tread a non-confrontational path. One, therefore, finds a clear road ahead on which to continue with one's journey as planned. On the other hand, when one opts for the violent method, the journey ends in confrontation. In this case, one is faced at every moment with obstacles from the other side. This kind of journey is against the law of nature, hence it is doomed to failure. According to the Creator's scheme of things, every person is free to make his own choices. This means that the road of life is not one-way-traffic. At every moment, other vehicles are coming from the opposite direction. So, one has to be able to deal with this onrush of vehicles. It is this art of journey management which is called peace.

Given this state of affairs, the only way to ensure success is to adopt a two-fold strategy in one's planning, that is, endeavouring to pursue one's personal agenda while at the same time adjusting with the activities of others. This may seem like walking a tightrope, but it can be done with proper planning.

In this world a person can exercise his freedom in whichever way he wants, but he cannot change the Creator's scheme of things. A person has only two choices—either he should adjust to the divine plan and be successful, or go against it and be ready to face failure. There is no other option for anyone.

A man who was once very fond of trees wanted to see a green tree in the courtyard of his home. He thought that if he planted a sapling, it would take a long time to grow into a tree.

So, he went to a garden and selected a fully grown tree. He then employed several labourers to dig it up and then transport it to his courtyard where he had it planted.

> *A person has only two choices—either he should adjust to the divine plan and be successful, or go against it and be ready to face failure.*

The man was very happy. He thought to himself: 'I have travelled a long journey in a single day. Planting a sapling or a seed would have been a lengthy business and now I have found a quick way of having a lush green tree.'

But the next morning, when he looked at the tree, he found that its leaves had begun to wither, and after a few days the whole tree dried up. He was naturally disappointed. When one of his friends visited him, he found him in a very sad mood. When he asked the reason, he said: 'I am in a hurry, but God isn't.'

This story tells us that anyone who goes against the law of nature will never have success in his endeavours. This law of nature is applicable not only to trees: it is a universal law. In every field, one must follow this natural course; otherwise one cannot attain any worthwhile goal.

This principle also applies to the terrorist culture. This kind of culture will always fail, although the perpetrators of terror acts may justify their actions in very beautiful terms. Before undertaking any task, a person should always think whether or not his planning is in accordance with the law of nature. If it is, then he will be successful, otherwise he is doomed to failure.

The Policy of Mutual Non-interference

The estimated number of stars in the universe is 100 octillion or 10 to the power 29. The number of planets in the universe is around 10 to the power 24. These numerous stars and planets are constantly on the move in the vast universe. This has been going on for billions of years. For example, the earth is continuously revolving around the sun. Similarly, the other planets constituting the solar system move around the sun in their respective orbits. For billions of years, these celestial bodies have been following their specific paths, without interfering in the motion of or clashing with each other.

It is true that several collisions have occurred in the universe. But these phenomena are designed for the sake of the purposeful evolution of the universe which is continually evolving and expanding. These processes are always well-planned and meant to serve a useful purpose.

The harmony that characterizes the universe is mentioned thus in the Quran with reference to the earth and the moon:

> 'It is He who created the night and the day, and the sun and the moon, each [peacefully] gliding in its orbit.' (21:33)

It is this policy of mutual non-interference that has established total peace in the vastness of space.

This is the culture of the macro world. The same culture is also in evidence in the micro world. The atom, a tiny unit of the material world, has within it the same culture. An atom consists of a number of tiny particles, each one of which is constantly on the move. But there is no clash. So, there is the same peace in the micro world as we see in the macro world.

There are about 50 million large and small animal species on the earth. Again there is total peace in the animal world. Wars such as the First World War and the Second World War have never occurred in the animal world. All these living creatures engage in numerous different activities. How is it then that there is total peace? The answer is that animals have also adopted the same culture—that of mutual non-interference. The only difference is that what the material world has adopted under the law of nature, has been adopted by the animal world as a result of its inborn instinct.

Every person is free to launch his or her own activities, the only restriction being that he or she should not become harmful for his or her fellow beings.

The same culture—the culture of mutual non-interference is also required in the human world. Every person is free to launch his or her own activities, the only restriction being that he or she should not become harmful for his or her fellow beings. In other words, human beings also have to adopt the same culture, that is, the culture of mutual non-interference. This is the only formula for peace based on the law of nature.

The culture of mutual non-interference brings peace, and peace opens up the door to all opportunities. And by utilizing these opportunities, everyone can achieve his or her goal. In other words, everyone has the chance to turn his or her potential into actuality.

This is the law of nature. And it is this law of nature that has been adopted in Islam. Here, I will give two relevant references. Before the Hijrah or migration (622 AD), when the Prophet of Islam was in Makkah, this verse was revealed in the Quran:

'For you your religion, for me mine.' (109:6)

After the Hijrah, when the Prophet settled in Madinah, he confirmed this principle. At that time roughly half of the population of Madinah comprised of Jews and the other half of Muslims. The Prophet issued a historic document called the Madinah Declaration, in which he proclaimed: *Lil-yahudi dinuhum wa lil-muslimina dinuhum.* This means,

'For Jews their religion and for Muslims their religion.'[1]

This principle, that is, the policy of mutual non-interference is based on an eternal principle, which is already established in the non-human world. It is also a matter of necessity in the human world.

This culture will also be adopted by the people of Paradise, as has been stated in the Quran in these words:

'And God calls to the Home of Peace.' (10:25)

The policy of mutual non-interference gives every man and woman the scope to live on his or her own without inflicting harm on other fellow human beings. This is the only formula for peace and harmony.

Mutual non-interference ensures that every person has an equal opportunity to make progress. This culture has been established throughout the entire universe, the only difference being that, in the non-human world, it is in place under the law of nature, while man adopts this culture of his own free will, without any compulsion. Man's thinking is involved in the choice he makes, therefore, the phenomenon of intellectual development is found only in the human world and not in the non-human world.

The 'Save Yourself' Formula

❦

According to the Bible, Jesus Christ said:

'Whoever takes away your coat, do not withhold your shirt from him either.'[1]

This does not mean to surrender to your rival, but simply to engage in wise planning. This saying embodies a great piece of wisdom. By adhering to this policy, great success can be achieved in life.

When at the time of controversy, you agree to offer your "shirt" to someone, you save your time and energy as a result. It is a kind of 'buying time' strategy. This is a formula for wise planning.

It is not "shirt" that matters. The most important issue is that in every situation there are enormous opportunities. If you entangle yourself in the problem of the "shirt"—that is, someone wants your shirt and you are not willing to give it away—you will then certainly remain unaware of all the other aspects of the situation. In particular, you will not be able to see the abundance of opportunities all around you. Due to this negative involvement you will lose your positive thinking.

There are evidently far greater arenas for action than fighting for a "shirt". In such a situation, if you prevent your mind from succumbing to negativity and try to reflect on the issue with positivity, then you will realize that the real problem is not to keep the "shirt" in your hand, but to avail of the opportunities around you.

The above saying of Jesus Christ is a maxim of universal application. All the prophets adopted this strategy, in one form or another, and on each occasion this method proved to be successful.

For example, ancient Makkah was the home town of the Prophet Muhammad. At that time the leaders of Makkah forced him to leave the city and settle elsewhere.

The Prophet duly left Makkah and migrated to Madinah. This was like giving away the "shirt" at the time of an unjust demand. But the Prophet accepted this with a positive mind. At the time of his migration, he said:

'I am told to opt for a town that will swallow all other towns.'[2]

The implication of this saying was: 'If I fight with the Makkan leaders on this issue, I will be wasting my time and energy. But if I leave Makkah and settle in some other town, there will be enough time for me to re-plan peacefully for my mission.'

The secret of success in life is not to make others suffer losses at your hands. The secret of success in life is to plan one's time and energy wisely and to avail of the opportunities within one's reach.

The Prophet quietly migrated from Makkah without any protest and settled in Madinah. He adopted the peaceful method for spreading his mission. The result of his devoting himself entirely to this peaceful agenda was miraculous: without fighting, he was able to conquer the hearts of people. It has been proved that when the heart is conquered, everything else is also conquered.

The secret of success in life is not to make others suffer losses at your hands. The secret of success in life is to plan one's time and energy wisely and to avail of the opportunities within one's reach. All this should be done in a silent manner. The result of this peaceful strategy on the part of the Prophet Muhammad was that seven years after his migration from Makkah, he was able to organize a peaceful march to Makkah and enter the city without facing resistance from his opponents. This event is mentioned in Chapter 110 of the Quran.

At the time of controversy people generally fight with others. But this is not a wise course of action. The wise course is to avoid fighting and strive to reach your goal through quiet planning, all the while keeping a low profile. One should discover the available opportunities and try to peacefully utilize them. This is the law of nature, and the law of nature never fails. If you follow this strategy based on the law of nature, you will certainly have success.

The Policy of Delinking

❦

The British educator E.E. Kellet (1864 – 1950) writing about the Prophet Muhammad in his book, *A Short History of Religions*, observes,

'He faced adversity with the determination to wring success out of failure.'[1]

What was the method which led the Prophet to this unusual success? It was adherence to the policy of delinking two issues. One example of this is when in 610 AD the Prophet Muhammad began his mission in Makkah, a town of Arabia, to propagate the ideology of monotheism – that is, believing in the one God and worshipping Him alone. It was the first quarter of the seventh century and in those times the Arabs were mostly idol worshippers.

Four thousand years prior to this, the Prophet Abraham had built a mosque in Makkah in which to worship the one God. It is this mosque which is called the Kaaba. But, in later periods, idol worshippers belonging to various Arab tribes began to place their idols in the Kaaba until, finally, the total number of idols within the precincts of the Kaaba reached no less than 360.

From the point of view of his mission, this was the greatest problem faced by the Prophet Muhammad. Apparently, what he should have done was to begin his mission by purging the Kaaba of idols, even if he had to engage in a violent confrontation with the custodians of the Kaaba.

But the Prophet Muhammad analyzed the situation dispassionately and came to the conclusion that the presence of idols in the Kaaba, although ostensibly a negative factor, also had a positive side to it—that is, because these idols belonged to different tribes of Arabia, people from all over Arabia would come to Makkah all the year round to visit their idols. Therefore, almost on a daily basis, in and around the Kaaba, there would be gatherings of substantial numbers of people. The Prophet Muhammad adopted the policy of delinking two issues: the presence of idols in the Kaaba and the gathering of people there. He decided to temporarily ignore the problem of the presence of idols in the Kaaba and to avail of the gathering of visitors there as an audience for his mission.

The Prophet adhered to this policy of delinking for a period of thirteen years, until finally a substantial number of Makkans became his companions. It is this wise strategy which has been described by E. E. Kellet in these words: He faced adversity with the determination to wring success out of failure. In other words, the Prophet adopted this formula for his mission: Ignore the problems, avail of the opportunities.

The principle adopted by the Prophet Muhammad in ancient Makkah was not, in fact, a religious principle. This principle was based rather on the law of nature. According to the general law of nature, this principle applies to everyone, whether one's mission be religious or secular.

The truth is that, according to the law of nature, always in every situation two things exist at the same time – problems and opportunities. It can never happen that one aspect should exist and the other not—that is, that problems should exist and opportunities should not. That is why wisdom dictates that before embarking on a mission, a person should review the situation in a dispassionate way, and refrain from launching himself on a course of action with an eye only on the problems, for this is a way of proceeding which goes against nature.

The principle of delinking helps a person to save himself from opting for violent methods when utilizing peaceful means will achieve his goal.

In this world the only practicable method is that which is based on positive planning: that is, ignoring the problem and discovering the opportunities present, and then availing of them. According to the law of nature, this is realistic planning. And in this world, realistic planning alone is successful so far as the result is concerned.

In this world the only practicable method is that which is based on positive planning: that is, ignoring the problem and discovering the opportunities present, and then availing of them.

In present times, those who are involved in violence show that they are unaware of the principle of success based on the policy of delinking. Since these people are going against the law of nature, they can never be successful in this world. They are fated only to carve out a history of destruction. They can never create a history of progress and development. The eternal law of the Creator for this world is that the way of violence never works and that only the way of peace is feasible.

Result-oriented action in this world is that which is based on peace. The method based on violence will always be a failure, just as a farmer would be unsuccessful if he dropped a bomb on his field and then expected lush green vegetation to flourish there.

The Power of Peace is Greater than the Power of Violence

Subhas Chandra Bose (1897 – 1945) was a great leader of India. The goal he had set for himself was to free India of the British rule. He gave this slogan to Indians: 'Give me blood, and I shall give you freedom.'

The Indian people gave him blood in the form of the Azad Hind Fauj (Indian National Army). However, this strategy completely failed. Subhas Chandra Bose himself died in an accident before he was able to fulfil this goal.

Mahatma Gandhi emerged as the true leader of the Indian freedom struggle. But he opted for a different course to achieve his goal—that of peace. His slogan for his people was: 'Help me in my non-violent activism, and I will give you freedom.'

Gandhi's peaceful strategy worked and India successfully won its freedom on August 15, 1947.

The strategy of Subhas Chandra Bose was based on violent struggle. This strategy was bound to provoke counter-violence from the British rulers, who were in a much stronger position. Therefore, Subhas Chandra Bose's strategy failed to work and British rule stayed in place.

Mahatma Gandhi's approach was the opposite. When he declared that he would continue the freedom struggle – but by the power of peace and not by the power of violence, the British rulers lost all justification for their violence. It is said that after Gandhi's announcement, a British collector sent the following message to his secretariat by telegram: 'Kindly wire instructions how to kill a tiger non-violently.'

The above experience of Indian politics shows that the power of peace is far greater than the power of violence.

A parallel historical example is that of the Prophet Muhammad, who started his mission in 610 AD in Arabia. At that time Arabia was tribal in its culture. Due to the conditions prevalent in that age, there were initially some violent clashes between the Prophet and his opponents, and the situation remained unsettled.

However, the Prophet wisely managed to conclude a peace agreement, which has come down in history as the Hudaybiyyah Agreement (628 AD). This was a no-war pact between the two parties. Consequent upon the pact, the Prophet found ample opportunities to further his mission by engaging in peaceful activity. The result proved to be miraculous: within just a few years, the whole of Arabia had accepted his ideology.

The American writer Michael H. Hart acknowledges the Prophet Muhammad as the supremely successful man in history.[1] But, what was the secret of this supreme success? It was certainly 'peace'. By dint of wise planning, the Prophet established peace in Arabia, and this allowed him and his companions to avail of the opportunities that were subsequently opened up. His miraculous success was due to this peaceful strategy.

The general policy of the Prophet is given in this Hadith:

'Whenever the Prophet had to choose between the two, he always opted for the easier course of action over the harder course of action.'[2]

Here, the easier course of action means the peaceful course and the harder course of action is the violent course. It was this policy followed by the Prophet that made him supremely successful.

Scope for peaceful planning exists everywhere and at all times. The sole prerequisite for this is patience. For it is patience which gives one the ability to analyze situations with an objective mind. When one is free of prejudice and predilection, one becomes a super-planner. Historians generally acknowledge that the Prophet Muhammad was an extremely successful person in world history, the reason for his great success being simply his clear-mindedness about planning along peaceful lines.

The target of the violent method is negative,
while that of the peaceful method is positive.

Why is peace more powerful than violence? The reason is that the sole objective of one who adopts the violent method is to make the rivals incur loss, while one who adheres to the peaceful method aims to make himself strong. The target of the violent method is negative, while that of the peaceful method is positive. It is a truism of life that however many losses one makes the other party suffer, it will never cause one to become strong oneself. The secret of success is to make one's own self strong, and this is possible only when one does not set a negative target for oneself, but rather moulds one's policies with a view to arriving at a positive outcome.

The Examples Set by Two Prophets

∽≈∽

Joseph was an Israelite prophet and Muhammad was an Ishmaelite prophet. Both are accepted among the Semitic religions and both were super-achievers.

The Prophet Joseph came to ancient Egypt around the seventeenth century BC. At that time the Hyksos Kings were the rulers of Egypt. A time came when a famine loomed large over Egypt, but Joseph devised a plan to save the country from starvation and at that point the then king of Egypt offered Joseph a high position in his government, that is, the administrator of storehouses of the land (*khazain al-arz*) (12:55). According to the Bible, the king said to Joseph:

'You will be over my house, and all my people will obey your commands. Only with regard to the throne will I be greater than you.'[1]

Joseph accepted the post offered by the king and perhaps continued in it till his death. The Quran refers to this story as *ahsan al-qasas*, or the best story. How did Joseph's story become the best story? It was through the application of wisdom. With the sovereignty of the country still in the hands of the king, the Prophet Joseph adopted the formula of political adjustment.

In the above Quranic verse, 'the best story' implies the best method. The course of action followed by the Prophet Joseph was that he never tried to unseat the king but accepted the political status quo which existed at that time. The result was miraculous. Joseph was able to command all the affairs of ancient Egypt without his being on the throne. It was this method that made his story 'the best story'. God has set this example through His Prophet so that the later generations may follow it and achieve success in the same way as the Prophet Joseph did.

The other story is that of the Prophet Muhammad. He started his mission in the first half of the seventh century in Arabia. At that time Arabia was a polytheistic region, and Makkah was the centre of this culture of idol worship.

When the Prophet Muhammad started his mission of *tawhid*, or monotheism, all the tribal leaders opposed him. They created all kinds of problems for him and his companions. Then in 628 AD at Hudaybiyyah, some ten miles from Makkah, the Prophet initiated negotiations to establish peace in Arabia. The tribal leaders were highly opposed to entering into any kind of peace agreement. The Prophet Muhammad, very wisely, accepted all the conditions presented by the opposite party and in return they finalized the Hudaybiyyah Agreement, which was a ten-year no-war pact.

After this peace agreement was concluded, normalcy was established in Arabia. Thereafter, the Prophet wasted no time and with wise planning set about spreading his mission in Arabia and its adjacent areas. The result was miraculous: in a few years, the whole of Arabia accepted his ideology. The Hudaybiyyah Agreement was an expression of the peaceful method, and by adopting this method the Prophet Muhammad emerged as the master of the situation in Arabia of that time.

The Prophet Joseph achieved success by accepting the king's constitutional authority and in return the king gave him an opportunity to manage all the affairs of the country in the political field.

The same method was adopted by the Prophet Muhammad, although in a different way. He accepted the political authority of tribal chiefs and tried, by wise planning, to avail of the opportunity presented in non-political fields. Again, the result was miraculous: the Prophet Muhammad emerged as the leader of Arabia.

The essence of both the methods is to not adopt the way of confrontation in the political field and to avail of the opportunities in the non-political fields. One will then certainly emerge victorious.

The Prophet Joseph's method is referred to in the Quran as the 'best story' (12:3). While the result of Prophet Muhammad's planning is referred to as a 'clear victory' (48:1). The essence of both the methods is to not adopt the way of confrontation in the political field and to avail of the opportunities in the non-political fields. One will then certainly emerge victorious.

The method followed respectively by the Prophet Joseph and the Prophet Muhammad was relevant not only in the past, but is applicable at all times, even today. For those who are engaged in violent activism in the present times, this method is also workable. This principle is thus a universal principle— no other principle is going to work in similar situations.

An Institutionalized Buffer

⚜

*D*uring the period when the Prophet Muhammad was in Makkah (610 to 632 AD), there was a war in 627 AD called the Battle of the Trench (*Ghazwa al-Khandaq*) in which the opponents of the Prophet Muhammad set out to attack Madinah. But due to the Prophet's wise management of the situation, no actual military confrontation took place.

The Prophet Muhammad's system of intelligence being highly organized, he received information that a formidable army of about 10,000 men was heading towards Madinah from Makkah, which was about 450 km away. The intention was to attack the city.

In conformance with his general policy, the Prophet judged it best to avoid any fighting. Therefore, after consulting his companions, he decided that the best course was to dig a trench outside Madinah. This was a very practical plan, because it had to be carried out only on the side of the city which was exposed to attack. The other three sides were impenetrable due to mountain ranges and densely planted date orchards. The Prophet and his companions then worked day and night for ten days to dig the trench, which was approximately 5,544 meters long, 4.6 meters wide and 3.2 meters deep.

When the Prophet's opponents had almost reached Madinah, they found this trench completely blocking their entry to the city. They were reduced to camping outside Madinah and then, after two weeks of indecision and frustration they were forced to retreat.

This was an example of the 'buffer strategy'. The trench, serving as a buffer between the two sides, had effectively stalled any military action.

Today, we are living in an age when the buffer strategy is once again available to us on a much larger scale. Now, in the United Nations, we have, in effect, just such a 'buffer' in the sense of its being geared to intervention between two antagonistic nations. Formed in 1945, it extended its membership to almost all of the countries of the world. And under Chapter VII of UN Charter, it was decided by consensus that if any nation attacked another, the UN would actively intervene. One example of its successful intervention was the occasion of Iraq's attack on Kuwait in 1990, thanks to which Kuwait was saved from destruction. The United Nations is thus a great blessing for all the nations of the world in that it serves as an institutionalized buffer.

The buffer strategy is a very effective way to prevent war. Where in the seventh century AD the buffer strategy was applicable only on a limited scale, in the twenty-first century it has become a highly organized way of preventing war. Now a universal norm, it covers all the nations of the world.

Now, modern civilization has developed a very new modus operandi to avert clashes, namely, that of peaceful dialogue. Through peaceful dialogue, with the help of modern technology, it is possible to divert a violent clash towards an intellectual discussion. This is another form of institutionalized buffer that has come into existence.

If one utilizes the buffer strategy when faced with impending clashes, it will cover almost all the attendant problems. The buffer strategy is one of the keys to establishing peace. But what is needed to properly avail of this formula is patience and wise planning.

No wisdom is needed to engage in violence. Any foolish person can do so. But establishing and maintaining peace do require a high level of sagacity and planning. One who knows how to tackle problems with wise planning will always choose to refrain from stooping to violence.

No wisdom is needed to engage in violence. Any foolish person can do so. But establishing and maintaining peace do require a high level of sagacity and planning.

Wisdom dictates that in any potentially explosive situation, a buffer should be used as a strategy to keep antagonists from embarking on a collision course. In earlier times this strategy could be used only in a very limited way. But now that there has been a universal institutionalizing of this strategy, the scope for its use has increased exponentially.

Moreover, major advances, especially in the field of communications, have greatly facilitated discussion and the exchange of ideas. Indeed, the liberalization of thought and the spread of modern education have now made it possible for all individuals and groups right across the globe to have recourse to this strategy.

Chapter Four
The Experience of History

Living between Idealism and Pragmatism

⟨⁓⟩

Philosophers and reformers in every age have been obsessed with the concept of idealism. Some have wanted to establish an ideal government, but they have failed. Some have tried to establish an ideal society, but again they have failed. Some have wanted to establish ideal justice in society, but in spite of all sacrifices they have failed.

What is the reason behind this general failure? It has rightly been said that the ideal cannot be achieved. The reason is that man is born with an ideal thinking mind, but the world we live in is less than ideal. Man is consumed with the desire for the ideal, yet is bound to live in a world that is far from being ideal. As an eminent scientist once rightly remarked that it appears that man has strayed into a world which was not made for him.[1]

Almost all the unrest in human society is traceable to this fact. All men and women want to live in accordance with their own thinking which is based on idealism, but the law of nature being as it is, they fail to achieve their goal. It is this difference between our sense of the ideal and reality which creates problems. People as a result become frustrated, then they begin to register complaints and protests, and finally turn violent, opting all too frequently for fighting as a means to achieve a goal which will always remain elusive in this world.

The only way to establish peace in this world is to accept the formula of pragmatism. It is the greatest wisdom to be content with pragmatic goals when the ideal goal is not achievable.

An illustrative example is that of Alexander the Great. He inherited the land of Greece and became its king. But this was less than ideal for him as what he wanted was to conquer the whole world. Thus he embarked in pursuit of his goal with his army, but history tells us that in 323 BC he died in Babylon, with an overwhelming sense of failure, when he was only 32.

For Alexander the Great, the government of Greece was a pragmatic option, but on a political whim, he opted for conquering the whole world. According to his way of thinking, his option was an ideal he strove towards, but according to the law of nature the ideal is not achievable. Had Alexander the Great adopted the pragmatic approach, he would have surely been successful, but because of the pursuit of an ideal he lost even what he had already attained, while what he had aimed for was never to be achieved.

The only way to establish peace in this world is to accept the formula of pragmatism. It is the greatest wisdom to be content with pragmatic goals when the ideal goal is not achievable.

In this world this has been the case of almost all human beings. According to a Japanese proverb, 'If you chase two rabbits, you will lose them both.' With a slight change in wording, it may be said that one who runs after the ideal goal, loses both the ideal as well as the practically achievable goal.

Because of this obsession, people generally suffer from stress. This stress increases to a point where one begins to engage in complaining and protesting. This phenomenon in turn leads frequently to violence. It is this psychology of the people which is the basis for violence. If people knew the law of nature in this regard, they would be able to live in peace themselves and also give to others the gift of peaceful living.

For example, it was Soviet Russia's dream to establish the Communist empire, because of which it also ended up participating in the Second World War. This was an unrealistic target for the Communist USSR. Had it opted for the practical target, communism would have not gone down in history as a philosophy that advocated the use of violent means to attain its goal of a classless society.

This principle also applies to those people who have adopted violence as a method. They have a self-styled goal in their minds—such as the eradication of oppression or the establishment of ideal justice. But their own experience shows that even after making numerous sacrifices over a long period of time, they have not been able to achieve anything at all. They have only written a history of destruction. If they gave up the violent method and adopted the peaceful method, they would surely be remembered in history as the people who followed the peaceful course to attain their goals.

Peaceful Planning on the Basis of Realities

⟬—※—⟭

*O*ne aspect of the creation plan is referred to thus in the Quran:

'We shall certainly test you with fear and hunger, and loss of property, lives and crops. Give good news to those who endure with fortitude.' (2:155)

This means that according to the creation plan of God, loss is an integral part of life, in both political and non-political spheres. Therefore, the right attitude to this is to accept loss as a reality and then plan peacefully for the future in non-confrontational fields. This is the only wise formula for success in this world. On the contrary, those who engage in planning in order to recover what they have lost are certainly doomed to failure.

For example, Pakistan was earlier a part of the Indian subcontinent. It was formed in 1947 after Partition with Muhammad Ali Jinnah (1876 – 1948) as its founding leader. However, the Pakistan Jinnah got did not measure up to his dream. In one of his speeches, he denounced the geographically truncated Pakistan.[1]

This statement of the founder of Pakistan became a trendsetter for all the Pakistani people. It then became the national policy of Pakistan to inveigh against the truncation of Pakistan.

According to their original proposal, Kashmir was to be a part of Pakistan, but after Partition, Kashmir became a part of India. This was not acceptable to the Pakistani leaders. The whole national policy of Pakistan revolved around making Kashmir a part of Pakistan. The former president of Pakistan, Pervez Musharraf, once said:

'Kashmir runs in our blood.'[2]

Because of this obsession, Pakistan has fought several wars with India. It has also initiated a proxy war against India. The so-called non-state actors of Pakistan are, in reality, crusaders for Kashmir. They have spent more than sixty years in trying to regain Kashmir but have not been successful in this endeavour. On the contrary, this strategy of Pakistan has proved to be counterproductive to the extent that in the eyes of the people of the world, Pakistan has become a failed state.

A contrasting example is that of Singapore. Singapore, earlier a part of Malaysia, separated from Malaysia in 1965 and became the independent republic of Singapore. Geographically, Singapore was also a truncated Singapore. But Singapore's founder leader, Lee Kuan Yew (1923 – 2015), was a very wise man in that he did not waste any time in trying to reverse the truncation of Singapore. Instead, he completely devoted himself to planning for his country's progress and development on the basis of the available resources. Within forty years after its formation, Singapore emerged as a developed country on all fronts.

Today the per capita income of Pakistan is 4,840 dollars, while that of Singapore is 76,860 dollars. Singapore is a debt-free country while Pakistan's international debt and liabilities have reached the alarming level at 65 billion dollars. Pakistan is placed eighth in the list of the most dangerous countries in the world, according to Country Threat Index (CTI) compiled on December 9, 2014 by IntelCenter, a Washington-based company working for intelligence agencies. Data released by the Economist's Intelligence Unit in January 2015 rated Singapore the second-most safe city in the world.

There is only one reason for this difference between these two countries. After its creation, Pakistan opted for violent activism and consequently paid a heavy price for it. Singapore, on the other hand, opted for peaceful constructive activities and is now reaping the best fruits of this peaceful policy.

The story of Palestine is similar. Palestine was partitioned in 1948 according to the terms of the Balfour Declaration. The Arabs saw Palestine as a truncated land and have been making enormous efforts to detruncate it. However, even after making great sacrifice they have not been successful. This is because their struggle was not against Israel, but rather against the law of nature. In this world, no one can expect to win a battle against the law of nature.

The advantage of peaceful planning is that because of it, the work of development begins from day one, while planning on the basis of unavailable resources means that development will remain a matter for the future.

In truth, success in this world can be attained only through peaceful planning. This means making plans on the basis of available resources. Planning on the basis of non-existent resources only leads to violence against supposed enemies, which leads to further losses. Experience shows that planning on the basis of available resources fosters a peaceful atmosphere.

The advantage of peaceful planning is that because of it, the work of development begins from day one, while planning on the basis of unavailable resources means that development will remain a matter for the future.

Planning itself is a peaceful activity which entails turning the potential into actuality. When you engage in planning, the entire process goes on in a peaceful manner. But when you try to reach your goal through violent means, you will never be able to arrive at your targeted goal. The law of nature is that one who begins with the right starting point reaches his target.

This principle applies to every individual, group and nation. Whoever engages in violent activism will never see his efforts fructify, because he did not begin his task in the right way. On the contrary, the individual or group which adopts the peaceful method will certainly arrive at the desired end, because their work was on the right lines from the very outset.

Terrorists may kill people with their guns and bombs, but they cannot repeal the law of nature. Changing the law of nature is beyond human capacity.

Violent Activism, Peaceful Activism

❧

*T*he English historian Edward Gibbon (1737 – 1794) observed in his famous work *The History of the Decline and Fall of the Roman Empire,*

> 'History is indeed little more than the register of crimes, follies, and misfortunes of mankind.'[1]

This is a negative remark. But every event of history, whether it be negative or positive, has a lesson for us. In this sense, it would be right to say that history is full of useful lessons. European politicians fought two wars: World War I (1914 – 1918) and World War II (1939 – 1945). The combined military and civilian casualties in these two wars numbered about 90 million. The economy of the continent suffered serious setbacks and constructive works such as education were severely hampered. Historians have never reported any positive gain resulting from these world wars.

In the same Europe there was another activity going on concurrently. This activity was conducted by scientists, educationists and other thinking people. The result produced by this second group was quite different: it culminated in glorious historical developments which brought to us heights of modern civilization till then unscaled.

The first group can be thought of as comprising violent activists, while the second group consisted of peaceful activists. Violent activism did not give anything to the world, either in the First World War or in the Second World War. On the other hand, for all mankind, peaceful activism ushered in a civilizational phase which was more highly developed than ever seen before.

If we examine both events by applying the criterion of the result achieved, we can safely conclude that after being witness to numerous examples from the past, there is no justification at all for adopting violent activism. It is high time for those who are engaged in violence to abandon this path forever. No individual has ever been known to have consumed poison twice. Similarly, there is no more justification for continuing with violence.

The game of fire and blood cannot be justified by describing it as a means of attaining justice. The truth about such people, both in the eyes of man and God, is that they are committing heinous crimes.

Those engaged in the gun and bomb culture in the name of religion have no justification for it in the present age. The negative effects of their violent culture are reported daily in the media, without any positive results ever being mentioned.

If those engaged in the violent culture were asked why they were following this course of action, they would say that it was to seek justice. But the truth is that resorting to violence is in itself the greatest form of injustice. This game of fire and blood cannot be justified by describing it as a means of attaining justice. The truth about such people, both in the eyes of man and God, is that they are committing heinous crimes.

People who indulge in violence in the present age are rightly called terrorists. Those who get killed in this violent enterprise are all innocent people. The Creator had created them to play a healthy role in this world, but the terrorists' actions have jeopardized this plan of God and have thus prevented them from playing the role required of them by their Creator. This attempt by the terrorists is undoubtedly the greatest crime, and criminals who perpetrate it can never earn God's forgiveness.

If a study of history is undertaken, it will be seen that human history is full of instances of war. In all cases, war has only led to the loss of life and the destruction of property. It can be said, then, that the first individuals who engaged in war could be forgiven, as they were unaware of its ill consequences. But those who continue in this way, even after realizing the negative experience of war, cannot be absolved of guilt.

As far as the modern age is concerned, war has become entirely irrelevant. This age is one of an explosion of opportunities—opportunities have increased to such a great extent today that everything one wants can be achieved by treading the path of peace. It would be true to say that, under the present circumstances, war and violence are no longer an option. What one failed to achieve in the past through confrontation can be successfully achieved in the present day and age solely by making use of peaceful means.

Following the peaceful method today is like letting a tree grow, while choosing the violent method is like cutting it down. Our task, then, is to grow a tree and not to cut it down – an indisputable axiom which is applicable not just to gardening but also in a highly significant way to human society.

A Prediction that Proved to be True

⟶ ※ ⟵

The Iraq War, an armed conflict that began with the March 2003 invasion of Iraq, was led by the United States during the tenure of President George Bush Jr. A military action, it was planned at the global level by the US. The US leaders were very hopeful of the results of this strategy. However, I had grave misgivings about this war and made a contrary statement about its possible result in an interview with a national daily long before the war was initiated. This interview was published with the title: *US Aggression would be Counter-Productive.*[1]

I made this statement not on the basis of some mysterious knowledge, but on the basis of long experience of history. It is a fact that throughout history it has never happened that the desired result could be arrived at through military action. This proved to be true for the wars waged by Alexander the Great (356 – 324 BC) and Adolf Hitler (1889 – 1945) and it applies likewise to all the warmongers of the present day.

It has been seen that not only does the side that loses face defeat, but even the winning side can only score a Pyrrhic victory, that is, a victory in which the victor's losses are as great as or even greater than those of the defeated. The phrase Pyrrhic victory is named after Greek King Pyrrhus of Epirus (318 – 272 BC), whose army suffered an enormous number of casualties in defeating the Romans at Heraclea in 280 BC and Asculum in 279 BC during the Pyrrhic War.

History repeated itself in the twentieth century in the case of the Second World War in which Great Britain was one of the major participants. When the war began, the British Empire was spread over so vast an area that, as the Scottish newspaper *Caledonian Mercury* once wrote,

'On her dominions the sun never sets.'[2]

But towards the end of the Second World War, Britain's strength became greatly diminished and, because of its inability to retain its control over the empire, it had no option but to set free all its colonies, including India, whose independence was announced by the British Viceroy Lord Mountbatten on August 15, 1947.

The example of war is like a plant with thorns, which will produce nothing but thorns when it grows into a tree. One who expects flowers from a thorn tree is living in a fool's paradise.

The greatest disadvantage of war is that its result is generally unforeseeable. In history no war has ever been fought whose consequence turned out to be exactly as expected. War is an entirely unpredictable game, one which causes little other than destruction. Thus, war is like jumping into a blind alley.

The case of peace is quite different. Peaceful planning inevitably produces the desired result. The example of war is like a plant with thorns, which will produce nothing but thorns when it grows into a tree. One who expects flowers from a thorn tree is living in a fool's paradise. Peace, on the other hand, is like a fruit-bearing plant which will yield fruits when it matures.

If the way of war and violence proved detrimental even in the earlier ages, the invention of weapons of mass destruction in the second half of the twentieth century has simply ruled out war as an option. Now the only option before an individual or group is that of peaceful struggle; violent struggle is not viable for anyone, even for the super powers.

If a person or group initiates war in the twenty-first century, they will prove that either they are completely unaware of the present realities or they have, because of some kind of false belief, made suicidal death their goal.

On the one hand, due to the development of technology, war in the present age has not remained an option for anyone. On the other hand, this same modern technology has opened up so many opportunities outside the battlefield that an individual can be hugely successful by simply treading the path of peace.

This historical change ought to be an eye-opener for all those who are involved in terrorist activities. Experience shows that till now their actions have not enabled them to gain anything positive. Their case is not an exception. This, too, will certainly be the case in the future. If extremists persist in terrorism, that will be tantamount to increasing their own losses.

Terrorists must realize that the sword may be named a 'flower sword', but it will not actually turn into a flower. Similarly, if the terrorists portray their acts as being designed to achieve a beautiful goal, even then they will prove to be unsuccessful. They must put an end to their violence without further delay and return to the path of peace.

Unending War

War on its own is an act which, once initiated, can never be brought to an end. If active war is discontinued, passive war takes its place.

In actual fact there are always two sides in a war: one winner and one loser. Either way, this does not bring about the end of war, for the victor becomes arrogant, as a result of which he overestimates himself. After the victory the winner's ambitions become very high. He now wants more and more success. This way of thinking perpetuates war, which then manifests itself in a number of destructive ways.

As for the loser, the psychology of defeat is such that one who is defeated is not ready to accept defeat, nor does he want to face another defeat. Failing to avenge his defeat is for him as bad as a second defeat. This is why the loser never accepts defeat. He wants to avenge his defeat, come what may.

For the smooth functioning of life, it is essential to put an end to the state of war. But history tells us that the will to end a warlike situation is produced neither in the victor nor the loser. This role has to be performed by a third party. With the intervention of a third party, there is always the possibility that the situation of war may be brought to an end.

For the smooth functioning of life, it is essential to put an end to the state of war.

We find an example of this when, in 1945 during the final stages of the Second World War, the United States dropped atom bombs on the Japanese cities of Hiroshima and Nagasaki. Japan felt an intense need to exact revenge for this most heinous crime carried out against the nation and in the process to teach America a lesson.

In those crucial times certain wise journalists and writers of Japan started a campaign in the country. They wrote powerful articles and books to pacify the Japanese people. They put forward the argument that if America had bombed their cities in 1945, they too had prior to this destroyed the United States' naval base at Pearl Harbour in 1941, and thus the scores had been settled. They further urged the people of their country to give up the path of revenge and to strive to build the nation anew. The Japanese paid heed to this wise advice and abandoned their desire for revenge. Instead they trod the path of cooperation with America. The result was soon there for all to see: Japan emerged as a highly developed country despite the destruction it had experienced during World War II.

The same situation prevailed between India and Pakistan. Pakistan was formed in 1947. From that time onwards rivalry between the two countries continued unabated. And then in 1971, India militarily joined the freedom movement of Bangladesh under the leadership of Sheikh Mujibur Rahman (1920 – 1975). As a result, Pakistan was subsequently partitioned. Several books were written on this issue, notably *Partition after Partition* and *The Dismemberment of Pakistan.*

This event generated great anger among the Pakistanis. During these delicate times, what was needed was for some wise thinkers to rise to the occasion and strive to pacify the Pakistani people. They should have made the Pakistanis realize that they had been instrumental in partitioning India in 1947 and that now India had helped to bring about the partitioning of their country in 1971. Thus, the scores were settled. It was now time to forget the past and build their nation along positive lines. However, no such thinker of Pakistan rose to the occasion. Consequently, Pakistan's hatred for India continued. It is for this reason that it has been involved in many negative activities against India. The result of these military engagements is that Pakistan has turned into a failed state.

It often happens among nations that war and violence break out. At such times, the groups at war are not able to turn their negative thinking into positive thinking by themselves. They cannot on their own abandon the path of violence in favour of the path of peace. What is needed at that time is that a third party should work to cool down their feelings of animosity and try to develop positive thinking in them. If there were people who could play such a role, then those at war could be brought back to the path of peace. But if no such attempt is made, then violence between the two groups goes on endlessly. This cycle of violence often does not end until both sides, in the process, completely annihilate each other, which is hardly the optimal way to end hostilities.

The Problem of Crisis Management

❧

*E*gypt and China faced the same kinds of international crises, but their respective responses and the subsequent results were different. China successfully managed the crisis, while Egypt failed to do so and paid a heavy price as a result.

Hong Kong, an island off the coast of China, was leased to Britain for 99 years according to the terms of a treaty drawn up in 1898. China wanted to regain the island, but it never took any steps towards achieving this goal on a unilateral level. It engaged rather in peaceful negotiations with Britain. After the completion of the 99-year lease, the United Kingdom, according to the agreement, restored all of Hong Kong to China on July 1, 1997. In this way the problem was settled peacefully.

The story of the Suez Canal of Egypt is quite different. The Suez Canal Company was created in 1858 to build and operate the Suez Canal. The relevant land was leased to it for 99 years from the time of the opening of the canal in 1869. After the 1952 coup in which King Farouk was overthrown, Gamal Abdel Nasser ruled as president of Egypt from 1956 to 1970. After some time as president, he announced the nationalization of the canal on July 26, 1956. But the 99-year lease granted to the Suez Canal Company still had twelve years to run. This provoked the week-long Suez Crisis. In retaliation, the UK, France, and Israel joined forces to invade Egypt and defeated the Egyptian forces. Later in the 1967 Six-Day War, Israel launched a massive air assault that crippled the Egyptian air capability. With air superiority it was able to control the Sinai peninsula within three days and then it captured Jerusalem's

Old City and gained control of the strategic Golan Heights on the Syrian border.

Both China and Egypt were faced with the problem of land lease to other countries. China was able to manage the crisis wisely, whereas Egypt was unable to do so. As a result, Israel captured large areas of Palestine which had earlier not been under its control.

Whereas Egypt had adopted the strategy of violent confrontation and then failed in its endeavour, China adopted a peaceful strategy and emerged victorious.

Life is full of crises—both for individuals and for nations. One who understands the art of crisis management is bound to be successful, while one who is unversed in this art is doomed to failure. The result of successful crisis management is peace, whereas failure in crisis management leads to war and violence.

All cases of war are nothing but instances of failure to manage crises. Conversely, all incidences of peace being maintained are the result of the successful management of crises by the relevant parties. Living in peace requires all concerned to learn the art of crisis management. On this score, there are no viable alternatives—neither for individuals nor for nations.

Life is full of crises—both for individuals and for nations. One who understands the art of crisis management is bound to be successful, while one who is unversed in this art is doomed to failure.

Crisis management calls for patience and wise planning. One who possesses these qualities will certainly be able to manage any crisis, however grave it might be.

When anyone manages a crisis, he has generally to pay the price of losing some right of his in the process. But this loss is quite temporary in nature and of lesser importance. The normalcy that returns after crisis management makes it entirely possible to regain what one had earlier lost—and often much more than what one previously had in hand.

In the present situation, any nation that is engaged in violence clearly demonstrates its incapacity to manage crises. Nations in this position need to reconsider their priorities and strive to develop a method of crisis management. If they continue with their violent policies, they will only increase their losses.

Violence—for anyone—is like getting into a quagmire, and the earlier one comes out of it, the better. One such example is the Vietnam War (1955-1975) in which the US was engaged for about twenty years. It ultimately had to acknowledge that its actions were not yielding the desired result, so it decided to unilaterally retreat from the battlefield. The US decision was a good example of the well-known idiom, 'Better late than never'.

Failure in crisis management leads to violence and war. In comparison, being successful in managing a crisis leads to peace. Crisis management requires patience. If a person proves to be patient in times of crises, his mind will function normally and very soon it will find a peaceful solution. On the contrary, if at the time of crisis a person loses his equanimity, his mind will not work efficiently, and will lead him to opt for the path of confrontation.

Maintain the Historical Status Quo

⟡

The only certain principle upon which to establish peace in society is that of maintaining the status quo. If one attempts to bring about a change in the status quo, this will almost certainly unleash violence. On the contrary, acceptance of the status quo brings peace to society.

The Kaaba is the holiest place for Muslims. It is believed that the Prophet Abraham built the Kaaba in Makkah in the second millennium BC, many centuries before the advent of the Prophet Muhammad. The form it takes today is that of a cube with a square base. However, when the Prophet Abraham first laid the foundation of the building, he gave its base a rectangular shape. The Kaaba continued in this shape until 600 AD when the people of Makkah undertook its reconstruction after it had been damaged by floods. In the process, they changed its shape, giving it a square base.

It was the mission of the Prophet Muhammad to revive the traditions of the Prophet Abraham. He did not, however, try to restore the Kaaba to the shape it had originally been built in by the Prophet Abraham. He left the Kaaba in its "truncated" shape.

The reason for this is given in a Hadith of *Sahih al-Bukhari*. That is, had the Prophet tried to change the shape of the Kaaba, a controversy would have erupted which might have affected the Prophet's peaceful mission.[1] That is why the Prophet left the Kaaba as it was in his time and did not make efforts to reshape it.

This prophetic Sunnah, or practice, gives us an important principle—that is, never try to change the historical status quo. Trying to make changes in any long-standing status quo will almost certainly lead to serious consequences, even including violence. There are a number of examples in the later history of Muslims which confirm the veracity of this principle.

Before its partition, Palestine came under the British Mandate for Palestine. The Mandate was a legal commission which functioned from 1923 to 1948 and formalized the British administration of the Palestinian territory that had formerly constituted the Ottoman Empire. The Mandate reaffirmed the 1917 British commitment to the Balfour Declaration, for the establishment in Palestine of a "National Home" for the Jewish people. In 1947 the United Nations proposed a Partition Plan for Palestine, which recommended the creation of independent Arab and Jewish States and a Special International Regime for the City of Jerusalem.

Arab leaders such as Hassan al-Banna, Sayyid Qutb, and Gamal Abdel Nasser refused to accept the partition plan. They wanted to reunite Palestine under Arab rule. But they completely failed.

The Palestinian "jihad" of the Arabs, despite immense sacrifices, only proved to be counterproductive. During this period, many opportunities were missed and numerous losses were incurred.

A status quo is never formed suddenly, but is established rather through the coming together or accumulation of several factors over a long number of years. Those who wish to change the status quo are never in a position to reintroduce favourable factors. These desired factors arise out of a long historical process; they cannot be brought into existence simply through political activism or agitation.

Peace is a positive state of affairs which can never be brought into being without positive planning. It does not come into being in a society all of a sudden: it requires wisely thought out, long-term efforts.

This is a historical reality. Accepting the historical reality in this regard will help in acceptance of the status quo, while not accepting this reality will lead one to try to change the status quo, which can never happen.

Peace is a positive state of affairs which can never be brought into being without positive planning. It does not come into being in a society all of a sudden: it requires wisely thought out, long-term efforts. War, on the other hand, is a negative event, which can take place without any kind of planning. Those who have the desire to establish peace in society must bear this point in mind, otherwise their efforts will be in vain – they will never fructify.

Trying to alter the status quo is not fighting against other human beings. It is rather fighting against historical laws. No person or group is so strong as to wage a war against history. Accepting the status quo is to accept history, whereas to try to change the status quo is tantamount to waging a war against history. In such a situation, a person has only one option, and that is, to accept historical realities and peacefully plan out his course of action, making use of whatever resources are available to him.

Lessons from History

According to the law of nature, the power of peace is greater than the power of war. The veracity of this principle has been confirmed time and again throughout human history. In particular, the experiences of the Second World War have valuable lessons to offer us on this subject.

Japan and Germany participated in World War II (1939 – 1945) with parallel ambitions. Japan's goal was to secure the position of the number one country of Asia, while Germany's aim was to become the number one country in Europe. The Second World War continued for six years, in the course of which both Germany and Japan were forced to sacrifice numerous lives and resources. Towards the end of the war, both countries had suffered massive and widespread devastation.

At the end of the war, leaders arose in both these countries, who in their wisdom, saved their people from becoming victims of negative thinking. For example, when the Emperor of Japan, Hirohito addressed his nation on the subject of the Japanese defeat on August 15, 1945, he said in a broadcast on Japan's national radio:

'It is according to the dictates of time and fate that we have resolved to pave the way for a grand peace for all the generations to come by enduring the unendurable and suffering what is unsufferable.'[1]

This message sent out by Japan's Emperor, aimed as it was at building a progressive future for the country, indicated a clear-cut line of action to the Japanese people. Thus Japan's post-war planning did not include preparations for revenge.

This peaceful planning worked, and within thirty years, Japan had emerged as the number one country of Asia.

Germany's modern history took a similar course. As the first post-war Chancellor of Germany (1949 – 1963) German statesman Konrad Hermann Joseph Adenauer (1876 – 1967) led his country from the ruins of World War II to being a productive and prosperous nation. A thorough statesman, who spearheaded Germany's intellectual leadership, he planned his country's future along peaceful lines – unlike his infamous predecessor, Adolf Hitler, who, with his aggressive tactics, had led Germany to defeat and ruination. With Adenauer's peaceful approach, Germany slowly recovered from the damages suffered during the war and eventually became the number one nation of Europe.

This experience of the twentieth century serves as an eye-opener for all those who still think in terms of violence and believe that they can achieve their goals by fighting. Islamic history is likewise replete with similar experiences.

In the thirteenth century, the Tartar and Mongol armies attacked the Abbasid Caliphate, destroying everything from Samarqand right up to Aleppo. In the process, there were some clashes between the Muslims and the Mongols, with the Muslims finally being subjugated. All their fighting had been in vain. The Muslims were so demoralized that it began to be said:

'Don't believe it, if someone says that the Mongols have been defeated.'[2]

Then, a new situation developed, with the Muslims abandoning violence under compulsion and becoming engaged in a peaceful mission. The British orientalist T.W. Arnold (1864 – 1930) in his book *The Preaching of Islam* reports that this peaceful process resulted in the majority of the Mongols accepting Islam.[3] Thus, the problem that could not be solved by war was solved through peace. Narrating this story the Lebanese American scholar Philip K Hitti (1886 – 1978) observes,

'The religion of the Moslems had conquered where their arms had failed.'[4]

This history of Islam sends out a strong message to Muslims—that is, having failed to achieve their goal through a violent struggle, the time has again come for Muslims to abandon all kinds of violence and attempt to achieve their goals by a peaceful method.

War depends entirely on the aggressive use of weaponry and can only be a source of destruction. Nothing constructive can be achieved through war and violence. On the contrary, peace, based on education and positive planning, inevitably leads to progress and development. The whole of human history testifies to this fact.

This history of Islam sends out a strong message to Muslims—that is, having failed to achieve their goal through a violent struggle, the time has again come for Muslims to abandon all kinds of violence and attempt to achieve their goals by a peaceful method.

War is perpetrated under the influence of negative thinking, and so its result is also negative. On the other hand, peaceful planning is engaged in under the influence of positive thinking. That is why the peaceful method invariably proves to be successful.

If studied objectively, history has valuable lessons for us. It has never been possible throughout history for anyone to achieve positive results through war, just as no one has ever obtained negative results by following a peaceful course of action.

History is a record of human experiences, both positive and negative. What is implicit in this record is the message that we should not repeat the negative experiences of history: we should repeat only those experiences which have led to positive results in the past.

Mankind's past has been recorded in books which are readily available in libraries across the world. Before rushing to the battlefield, the would-be combatants would be well advised to visit such libraries for guidance. Only after making a thorough study of the annals of history – which tells us about the negative and positive aspects of the events of human life over the past millennia – should they plan their future actions.

If you observe a garden with lush green trees, a mountain or an ocean; if you see the world of nature; if you see the starry universe, you will find that, everywhere, there is peace and tranquillity. It is only human life which is vitiated by violence and fighting. In this sense, man seems to be a creature at odds with the whole of the universe. If those who are engaged in militancy were to give some thought to this incongruity, they would feel ashamed of their conduct. They would immediately give up violence as a way of life and adopt the culture of peace.

A verse in the Quran gives this advice:

'Travel about the land and see what was the end of the deniers.' (6:11)

The implication here is that what happened to the deniers was not only unrewarding but also punitive and that a similar fate awaits those who engage in uncalled for militancy. It follows that one should study human history and then plan one's actions only after paying heed to its lessons.

Chapter Five

The Need for a Counter-Ideology

The Case of Present-Day Muslims

⚜

*I*t is said that Muslims all over the world are engaged in violence. Some Muslims are engaged in passive violence while others are engaged in active violence. Just thinking in extremist terms may be described as passive violence, while adopting the gun culture may be described as active violence.

This phenomenon pertains to Muslim practices and has nothing whatsoever to do with Islamic teachings.

The fact is that, according to the Quran, Muslims are witnesses of God before mankind, or *shuhada 'ala an-naas* (2:143). It was the same duty as was given to the Jews. As the Bible says:

'Therefore you are my witnesses, said the Lord.'[1]

In Chapter 3 of the Quran this fact is set forth in these words:

'God made a covenant with those who were given the Book to make it known to people and not conceal it. But they cast it behind their backs and bartered it for a paltry price.' (3:187)

The Jews were the People of the Book, but in the later period of their history they completely forgot their duty and discarded the concept of being witnesses. They replaced it with the concept of Jewish supremacism. Exactly the same has happened with the Muslims. They now think in terms of Muslim supremacism.

The Muslim thought that developed in the later period of Muslim history all stemmed from this notion of Muslim supremacism. It can be summed up as: *Nahnu khulafa Allah fil arz* (We are the vicegerents of God on earth).

Muslim literature of later days, directly or indirectly, projects this concept in a major way. And it is a concept which has been revived in modern times with even greater emphasis by two Muslim thinkers, the Egyptian Sayyid Qutb (1906 – 1966) in the Arab world and the Pakistani Sayyid Abul Ala Maududi (1903 – 1979) in the non-Arab world. It is this concept, popularized in the present century, which has ultimately led to terrorism in the name of jihad.

The present-day Muslim militants have adopted a self-styled concept of jihad, that is, to establish divine rule in the world, and have chosen to give their militancy religious justification by calling it jihad.

'Jihad' literally means 'utmost struggle'. The true interpretation of this word is 'a peaceful struggle for the dissemination of the message of God to mankind'.

The present-day Muslim militants have adopted a self-styled concept of jihad, that is, to establish divine rule in the world, and have chosen to give their militancy religious justification by calling it jihad. This is why the present Muslim militancy has gained so much ground. In other words, its proponents look upon it and project it as 'justified' militancy, or militancy based on ideology. To discharge this 'duty' they have – by their way of it – given legitimacy to all forms of violence, even suicide bombing.

Now the question is: how to tackle this militancy? The answer is that it requires a counter-ideology. The militants have purportedly legitimized their militancy by applying to it a wrong and misleading interpretation of the religious scriptures. We have to delegitimize it by replacing the wrong interpretation with the right interpretation. No other strategy will work.

Man is a rational animal. He always accepts things when his mind is properly addressed, and Muslim militants should certainly be no exception to this rule.

Here, I would like to narrate a very relevant story. Once on a visit to Palestine, I found some Arab boys singing a song in unison. One line of this was:

Halumma nuqatil halumma nuqatil fa inna al-qitala sabil ar-rashadi

(Let us make war, let us make war, for war is the way to success!)

I told them that it would be better if they sang like this:

Halumma nusalim halumma nusalim fa inna as-salama sabil ar-rashadi

(Let us make peace, let us make peace, for peace is the way to success!)

The Arab boys appreciated my suggestion and showed their readiness to fall in line with it. But then they said that they were surrounded by enemies. So, if they adopted peace, what would happen?

I explained to them: 'You have wrongly considered others as your enemies. They are not your enemies, but your *mad'u*, people to whom God's message has to be conveyed. According to the Quran (85:3), Muslims are *shahid* (witness) and all human beings are *mashhud* (the witnessed). Our duty is to convey the message of God to all mankind.' Then I pointed out to them that their violent method had not yielded any result, but that if they engaged in peaceful *dawah*, then God Almighty had promised all kinds of help for this work. As the Quran says:

'God will surely help him who helps His cause—God is indeed powerful and mighty.' (22:40)

The Arab boys were very pleased with what I had said and then one of them presented me with an olive branch from a nearby tree, as a token of peace. By taking into consideration human nature, it can be said that this experience is applicable to all the Muslims of the world.

It Requires a Literary Bomb

⬥

*M*ilovan Djilas (1911 – 1995) who was born in Yugoslavia, was influenced in his early youth by communism and became an active member of the communist party. Later in life, he rose to become the Vice President of the Federal People's Republic of Yugoslavia. But when he saw the practical results of communism, he became a strong critic of the communist regime.

In 1957, Djilas published a book, *The New Class: An Analysis of the Communist System*, in which he argued that communism in the Soviet Union and Eastern Europe was not egalitarian, and that it was establishing a new class of privileged party bureaucrats, who enjoyed material benefits from their positions. This book proved to be very successful and was translated into more than 40 languages.

Reviews on this book were written throughout the world. The *Reader's Digest* reviewed the book under the title: *The Book That Is Shaking the Communist World*.[1] America was strongly opposed to communist Russia, but rather than drop a nuclear bomb on it, it devised and supported a literary campaign against the communist regime. A sizeable number of books were published and disseminated in various languages which criticized the flaws in the philosophy of communism. All this had taken careful planning and amounted to throwing down a challenge to communism at the ideological level. This strategy was successful, and in 1991 the USSR collapsed after sixty-nine years of existence.

This is also the right way to tackle the modern-day so-called Islamic terrorist movements. The use of chemical or nuclear bombs is not the way to eradicate this kind of terrorism. It requires a literary bomb to encourage people to shun terrorism and follow the path of peace. In present times, tackling the menace of terrorism requires a powerful book on the subject, one which can again be reviewed under the heading: *The Book That Is Shaking the Terrorist World.*

There was a time when it was thought that Saddam Hussein was the biggest patron of modern Muslim terrorism. He was convicted on charges of killing and executed in 2006. After Saddam Hussein, Osama bin Laden, considered the principal leader spearheading terrorism, was likewise killed in 2011 when his hideout was bombarded. Then, Abu Bakr al-Baghdadi was regarded as the most formidable terrorist to be dealt with. According to media reports he was killed or seriously injured in an airstrike in November 2014.

The use of chemical or nuclear bombs is not the way to eradicate this kind of terrorism. It requires a literary bomb to encourage people to shun terrorism and follow the path of peace.

Yet, even after the killing of these leaders, terrorism, in the name of Islam, continues to flourish. This shows that we have to change our approach in this matter. We have to adopt a strategy other than the use of guns and bombs.

According to news reports, President Barack Obama all but admitted on June 10, 2015, the anniversary of the fall of Mosul, as he ordered an additional 450 military advisers to join the 3,500 already in Iraq, that his anti-IS strategy wasn't working.[2]

Going by experience, we ought, as far as this issue is concerned, to take a U-turn. We have to change our previous mindset if we are to put an end to the menace of terrorism. It is important to take lessons from historical experience. We have, therefore, to replace chemical bombardment with literary bombardment. This is the only way to success in this field.

Modern terrorism in the name of Islam is based entirely on the misinterpretation of Islamic texts. One example of this misinterpretation derives from a verse of the Quran, which says: *In al-hukmu illa lillah.* That is,

'All power belongs to God alone.' (12:40)

In this verse, *hukm* is used in the sense of the supernatural power of God. However, the Muslim extremist thinkers have misinterpreted it to mean political power. Furthermore, it is said that Muslims, as representatives of God, should establish God's rule on earth. This assumption is wrong because it is based on a Quranic verse which has been taken out of context.

Another verse in the Quran says: *'Idilu.* This means,

'Follow the principle of justice [in your life].' (5:8)

But a misinterpretation of this verse has taken it in the transitive sense instead of the original intransitive sense in which it was used in the Quran. That is, the verb used in the above verse does not have any direct object of action, but because it has been wrongly interpreted, it comes to have an object of action, which in this case is the outside world. Thus, the verse has been taken to mean that justice should be imposed on people by force. As a result of this misinterpretation, the concept of justice has been politicized, although this notion cannot truly be inferred from the text.

Any interpretation of the above kind is false. And this falsehood must be made manifest so that people may understand with certainty that the present militancy has no sanction in Islam and so that extremists will give it up, in the knowledge that their actions are un-Islamic.

The terrorist phenomenon is based on misinterpretation of the scriptures. It can be eradicated only by a right interpretation of the text being universally publicized.

In a speech on July 19, 2015, the British Prime Minister David Cameron expressing his anxiety about youngsters travelling to Iraq and Syria to join the Islamic State of Iraq and the Levant (ISIL), said,

'We must de-glamourise the extremist cause, especially ISIL. This isn't a pioneering movement – it is vicious, brutal, fundamentally abhorrent.'[3]

It is true that present Muslim extremism is the result of the glamourization of the self-styled concept of global Khilafat or caliphate. Its real solution lies in de-glamourizing this false ideology developed by extremists through a misinterpretation of Islamic sources. Moreover, de-glamourization of the Khilafat can be achieved by de-Islamizing this concept of the Khilafat based on false interpretation.

One of the aims of this book is to offer valid arguments to show that the concept of political Islam has no basis in Islam. It has to be conceded that the present concept of the false Khilafat is based on a political interpretation of Islam. This book demolishes the current false ideology of the Khilafat.

The UN has rightly adopted this dictum:

'Since wars begin in the minds of men, it is in the minds of men that the defences of peace must be constructed.'[4]

If we want to eradicate terrorism, we shall have to reengineer the minds of terrorists along peaceful lines. No other method will be of any avail.

Radicalization of Muslim Youths

⟜❦⟜

*P*resent-day Muslim militancy derives neither from the Quran nor the Sunnah. It is basically a product of the Muslim media—although this has come about unintentionally. The Muslim media since its inception to this day have been a vehicle for the launching of protests. And it is this protestant nature of the Muslim media that has formed the mindset of present-day Muslims. Muslim militancy and suicide bombing are mainly the consequence of this Muslim media.

The printing press was popularized in the Muslim world in the eighteenth century. Napoleon Bonaparte of France (1769 – 1821) was the first to introduce the printing press to Egypt when he invaded the country in 1798. That is to say, the printing press was brought to the Muslim world by the European colonial powers. It was a coincidence that the printing press came to the Muslim world at a time when they were witnessing colonial expansion in their lands.

Every day there was news of western powers encroaching upon the Muslim world, in one way or another. For example, in 1771 the Russian fleet totally destroyed the Ottoman Navy in the Mediterranean Sea during the Russo-Turkish War (1768-74). Sultan Tipu of Mysore was killed fighting the British army in 1799. The Mughal dynasty of India faced a crushing defeat at the hands of the British East India Company in 1857. The Italo-Turkish war between the Ottoman Empire and the Kingdom of Italy led to the capture by Italy of the Ottoman province of Tripolitania in 1912. Such events were bound to lead to repercussions in the Muslim community, which was further reflected in the Muslim press.

The Muslim world has been beset by such incidents from the eighteenth century right up to this day, and these events have been reported with exaggeration in the Muslim press.

In this way, the Muslim press has developed into a kind of protestant journalism. Now the electronic media is being used by Muslims towards the same end.

It is media of this kind that has created the Muslim mindset of the present day. The kind of thinking that characterizes Muslims in our times is not based on Islamic teachings, but stems rather from the Muslim media which invariably speaks the language of protests and complaints.

The Muslim militancy of the present age is based neither on reason nor on any teaching of Islam. It is entirely the upshot of the Muslim community's anger, disillusionment and negative thinking.

It is this pattern adopted by the Muslim media which has made Muslims negative. The Muslim community has therefore become an angry one and it is now directing its anger at other communities. When they saw that their gun culture was not producing the required results, they began, on account of their increasing anger, to indulge in suicide bombing in order to de-stabilize their supposed enemies.

The Muslim militancy of the present age is based neither on reason nor on any teaching of Islam. It is entirely the upshot of the Muslim community's anger, disillusionment and negative thinking.

It is said that the greatest menace of present times is the radicalization of Muslim youths. But the question is: What is the source of this radicalization? The Quran and the Sunnah are certainly not the ideological sources of this radicalization. The source of this culture is the use by Muslims of internet or social media as an extended form of Muslim media. Muslims have easy access to the international network—the internet, and are using it on a vast scale. Thus they have filled their websites on the internet with false pictures and false reports which show that Muslims are an imperilled community. This outreach of the social media is there in everyone's pocket in the form of mobile phones.

It is this website or internet culture that has basically contributed to the radicalization of today's Muslim youth. To save young Muslims from this negative culture, an extensive campaign is required to awaken Muslim minds in such a way that they may analyze information on websites on their own and develop the ability to differentiate between truth and falsehood. The present book is an attempt to aid them in this.

This kind of violence cannot be eliminated through counter-violence, because any counter-violence can only further aggravate the Muslims' anger. It is only due to this aggravated anger that they have taken to suicide bombing.

In the modern age, almost the entire Muslim community has started to lodge protests and complaints. Because of this mindset of theirs, Muslims have become receptive to negativity and not to positivity. Under the influence of this mindset Muslims tend to treat positive news with suspicion. All they know is that others are their enemies; they are unable to view people as creations of God. They only look at the negative aspect of events and fail to take account of their positive aspects.

Muslims today have coined a new term, that is, Islamophobia. This means that the West has wrongly come to regard Islam as danger to non-Muslims. This, however, is not actually the case.

I think this term would be more apt with a slight change. That is, the term should be 'Muslimophobia'.

Muslims have adopted the culture of violence in the name of Islam. In this sense the West is right to consider Muslims to be dangerous. Yet Islam, in itself, is a great blessing from God for the whole of humanity. But the present Muslims, due to their wrong interpretation of their own religion, have misinterpreted Islam as a religion of violence.

Muslimophobia addresses Muslims rather than anyone else. It is telling Muslims to abandon the wrong interpretation of Islam and shun the gun and bomb culture, so that people may be saved from developing misunderstandings about Islam. In this way, people will be able to have a positive understanding of God's blessing which has been sent for them by God in the form of Islam.

In view of the present situation, the question is, where is the silver lining? In the modern age Muslim reformers should focus on the Muslim youth. In his early, formative years, a person is relatively free from conditioning and is thus in a position to view things objectively and examine events in an unbiased manner. Our efforts should begin by trying to inculcate positive thinking in Muslims while they are still very young.

The new generation of Muslims is our hope, especially those who are availing of modern education. Modern education is helping in their de-conditioning. They are able to see the world in a more objective way and are developing the ability to understand things in a more realistic manner. It is these Muslim youths who are our hope for the future.

The Evil of Selective Information

⟨ ·//· ⟩

The printing press and electronic communications have ushered in a new age which has generally come to be called the age of information. But the question arises: why is it that the age of communication has brought along with it the age of hatred?

It is evident that people of almost every group, with the exception of the scientific community, have nothing but hatred for each other. The reason for this is the selective information placed in the public domain by writers and speakers. Every group, according to its interests, gives out only selective information for one reason or the other. That is, its reporting about the group which it considers its rival is one-sided. Human rights activists, social reformers, political leaders, media reporters, professional writers, and so on—almost all are, more or less, engaged in this practice.

One-sided reporting of this kind has made certain groups unsympathetic towards certain other groups. Under normal circumstances, this feeling lies dormant. But, it all too often flares up and takes on the form of violence and terrorism. The present-day terrorism is certainly a result of this phenomenon.

In the practice of one-sided reporting, the Muslim community is involved to a much greater extent than other communities are. Two examples illustrate this point. The first is of a book authored by the Syrian Muslim scholar Shaykh Abd ar-Rahman Hasan Habannaka al-Maydani. He has compiled several books in the Arabic language with the title, *Silsilah A'daa al-Islam* (*Series on the Enemies of Islam*, 2000).

The title of one book in this series is *Ajniha al-Makar ath-Thalatha wa Khawafiha* (*The Three Wings of Conspiracy and their Secondary Feathers*). In this book he mentions three anti-Muslim conspiracies at work to destroy Islam and Muslims. According to the author, these three conspiracies are: the Christian Mission (*at-tabshir*), Orientalism (*al-istishraq*) and Colonialism (*al-isti'mar*).

However, this kind of labelling is completely unjustified for those targeted by this author are not conspirators. Their activities are purely representative of the concerned groups' point of view. Each group has its point of view just as Muslims have their point of view. The above kind of labelling is the result of a lack of objectivity in viewing these factors and typifying them in a selective manner. If others also look at Muslims' activities in a selective manner, then they too would think that Muslims were involved in conspiracy. For example, a survey reported by the media said that Islam was the fastest growing religion in the UK.[1] If taken in a selective way, others would tend to think that Muslims were involved in a conspiracy to Islamize Britain. But if this trend is explained in terms of people's exercising their freedom of choice, it will appear to be a normal development.

In the nineteenth and twentieth centuries, certain historical developments took place, chief among them being Zionism, colonialism, communism and American expansionism. Muslims wrongly supposed that these were anti-Islam. Due to this wrong supposition, they started fighting against these forces and, to justify their actions they related them to Islam, declaring that Islam was in danger. But this was not true. Muslims should not have taken these changes as anti-Islam. They should have taken them as normal phenomena. It is a wrong supposition on the part of the Muslims that has created the problem.

If Muslims are free to engage in their activities, then they must allow others, too, to enjoy the same freedom. If Muslims give the title of conspirators to others, then they shall also have to give others the right to regard them as such. If Muslims have some reservations, they have the right to make a rational analysis of others' statements, but they do not have the right to label others as conspirators. Doing the latter is little better than resorting to abusive language.

It is not possible to change these writers' and speakers' proclivities. However, we can educate people so that they do not become provoked but ignore such events and reports, and refrain from allowing their thinking to be adversely affected.

This was an example from the medium of the printing press. Now, consider an example which was reported extensively both in print and the electronic media. A Muslim chaplain, Tahera Ahmad, of Chicago's Northwestern University was on board a United Airlines flight on May 30, 2015. During the flight she asked for an unopened can of soda and says she was told, 'Well, I'm sorry. I just can't give you an unopened can, so no Diet Coke for you.' When the man next to her got an unopened beer can from the in-flight service, Ahmad said she was told by the flight attendant: 'We are unauthorized to give unopened cans to people, because they may use it as a weapon on the plane.' On her Facebook page, Ahmad claimed this flight attendant was "discriminating against me." She used the hashtag *Islamophobia is real* for the post. Muslim activists then took to the social media to brand the alleged incident as an inexcusable act of bigotry and said they would boycott

United Airlines, basing their decision on what they interpreted as open discrimination.[2]

This incident is so trivial that it was almost a non-event, but posted as it was on Facebook by the above Muslim passenger, it became sensational news for the media, and was reported on a large scale. It is such reporting which appears in the media almost on a daily basis, which has developed hatred among Muslims for other communities, especially those of the West.

This kind of selective reporting is the greatest problem of the present times, in that it has spread negative thinking across the world. The Muslim authors and reporters who spread such news have become trendsetters for Muslims. These trendsetters are the ones who are responsible for the Muslims' present state.

It is not possible to change these writers' and speakers' proclivities. However, we can educate people so that they do not become provoked but ignore such events and reports, and refrain from allowing their thinking to be adversely affected.

Everyone enjoys freedom in this world. We cannot take away people's freedom, but certainly we have the wisdom not to form opinions on the basis of wrong reporting. We should form opinions based on our own reasoning.

Suicide Bombing

⌐—✽—⌐

*I*n the present day, suicide bombing is a unique and terrible manifestation of violence. The deadliest instance of such violence took place in New York, commonly referred to as 9/11, when the famous Twin Towers of the World Trade Centre (WTC) were destroyed by a group of Muslim militants. They hijacked four passenger airplanes, two of which were flown into the towers of the WTC. The attack resulted in the death of about 3,000 people and brought down the 110-storey buildings, besides causing severe damage to surrounding buildings and structures.

It is apparent that Muslims top the list of those using such deadly methods of suicide bombing. Yet, suicide is completely forbidden in Islam. According to a tradition recorded in *Sahih al-Bukhari*, a Muslim having been badly injured in a battle, could not bear the consequent pain, so he killed himself with his own sword. This was the first case of suicide in Islam. The Prophet said of this person to his companions that he would be among the people of Hell.[1]

According to Islamic texts, suicide is clearly an unlawful act. This being so, how has it come about that Muslims have established large organizations which train young people to carry out such suicide attacks? A great amount of funding is required for such activities. And, it is Muslims who are funding them. Thus, in this organized activity the whole Muslim community is, directly or indirectly, involved. A saying of the Lebanese-American writer Khalil Gibran (1883 – 1931) applies in this case:

'A leaf does not fall without the silent consent of the tree.'[2]

The root cause of suicide bombing is that in present times, the Muslim community has come to think of the world as being divided between Muslims and *kafirs* (non-believers); that, besides Muslims, everyone else is *kafir*; that the countries ruled by Muslims are *dar as-salam* (Land of Islam) whereas the countries ruled by people other than Muslims are *dar al-kufr* (Land of Disbelief). Due to this mindset, Muslims think that any heinous act may be perpetrated with impunity against supposed disbelievers.

It is because of this negative mentality of the Muslims of the present day that the ulama, or Muslim scholars, have become emboldened to publicly declare suicide bombing as lawful – an act which has always been unlawful in the absolute sense.

Moreover, there are certain Muslim scholars who have gone to the extent of openly issuing *fatwas*, or verdicts, claiming that suicide is lawful. They have coined a new term—*istishhad* (to seek martyrdom)—to give justification for suicide bombing.

Such *fatwas* are undoubtedly wrong. And it is strange that the entire community of religious scholars has not openly condemned this patently wrong *fatwa*.

The method of suicide bombing – known as hara-kiri – was first adopted in a big way by Japan. Traditionally practiced in that country, it was a ritual form of suicide carried out by slashing one's abdomen. As we know, the method of hara-kiri adopted by Japan in the Second World War turned out to be totally ineffective, and it was subsequently abandoned.

The practice of suicide bombing by Muslim militants has likewise become totally ineffective. By such attacks, they put an end to innocent lives, but this fails to produce any positive results. The question then arises as to why this deadly method of suicide bombing still continues.

The reason is that Muslims on their own have developed a baseless belief that a believer killed in a battle becomes a martyr, and therefore goes straight to heaven. This is a false belief. According to Islamic teachings, there is absolutely no doubt about the fact that those Muslims who kill themselves in suicide bombing will die an unlawful death. No heaven is waiting to welcome them.

Islam believes that the whole world including the Muslim world is *dar al-insaan* (the abode of human beings). It is Muslims' bounden duty to regard all human beings as God's creatures. Once, in Madinah, the Prophet of Islam, on seeing the funeral procession of a Jew, stood up in deference to it. When one of his companions asked him why he did so, he replied:

'Was he not a human being?'[3]

The Prophet Muhammad thus recognized a commonality between himself and a Jew—that the God who had created him had also created the Jew. This is the real basis of human equality.

According to Islamic teachings, there is absolutely no doubt about the fact that those Muslims who kill themselves in suicide bombing will die an unlawful death. No heaven is waiting to welcome them.

Today the armament industry is one of the most flourishing enterprises in the world. The question is, who has turned the armament industry into a flourishing business? It is clearly the buyers of arms who have done so. These customers are God's creation and God gave them minds so that they might use it for a healthy purpose. But they have instead used them for a destructive purpose, which is against the divine will. The Creator will ask them about how they used their minds—to a constructive end or a destructive end? The Creator will point out to them that He had given them their precious minds to be used for constructive purposes, but they used them instead for destructive purposes. Will they have any answer to this?

It All Depends on
the Angle of Vision

⌒✴⌒

The English poet and religious writer Frederick Langbridge (1849 – 1923) says in one of his poems:

'Two men looked out from prison bars, one saw the mud, the other saw the stars.'[1]

In looking at any event, there are evidently different angles from which to view it. The opinion one forms depends upon one's standpoint. Viewing from one angle can make a person positive, while viewing from another can make him negative.

This phenomenon is aptly illustrated by the event of 9/11 in the USA. Certain Muslims, who viewed America from the negative point of view that it was an enemy of Islam, wanted to teach it a lesson by carrying out a suicide attack on its soil. On September 11, 2001 a group of terrorists hijacked four passenger airplanes, two of which were crashed into the North and South towers of the World Trade Centre complex in New York City. Both the 110-story towers collapsed and the resulting fires caused extensive damage to surrounding buildings in the WTC complex.

Some time after the attack on the World Trade Centre, I participated in a conference of the Nuclear Disarmament Forum held in Zug, Switzerland on October 12, 2002. In the speech which I made on that occasion, I referred to the horrendous September 11 attacks and while speaking about this incident, I started to cry. I also wept in my office in New

Delhi when on the radio I first heard about the attacks the day they were carried out.

The reason I cried is that I realized that those who were involved in the perpetration of this act of violence were completely lacking in wisdom. They looked at the WTC from a negative angle. But had they seen it from a positive angle, they would have learnt a great lesson.

I had gone to New York in February 1998. During the visit, I also went into the World Trade towers and climbed to the top. Where the terrorists had seen these towers negatively, I viewed these buildings from a positive angle and was thus able to discover a great piece of wisdom from this observation. I reflected that modern technology was a great gift of nature, as it had opened up a new scope for people, that is, if there is not enough land for horizontal growth, one can always compensate for it by vertical growth.

The Quran was revealed in the seventh century, long before the advent of modern civilization. At that time the Quran made a historical prediction about the future in these words:

'We shall show them Our signs in the universe and within themselves, until it becomes clear to them that this is the Truth.' (41:53)

This means that after the revelation of the Quran, a revolutionary process was to be initiated in human history. The twentieth century was a culmination of this developmental process.

The twin towers of the WTC, a symbolic illustration of this new development in history, represented a whole new age. In former times, only horizontal growth had been possible. But now due to advances in technology, unlimited vertical growth had become a reality. These towers were thus symbolic of God's unique blessing on mankind. However, because certain Muslims wrongly considered them to be a symbol of their supposed enemy, they destroyed them in an unusual air raid of unprecedented destructiveness.

The above historical prediction of the Quran has manifested itself in numerous ways in the present age. For example, in ancient times, the marvels of God's creation could only be vaguely discerned with the naked eye, whereas today they can be observed in far greater detail and to a much greater degree of magnitude, due to the invention of the telescope and the microscope.

In the previous ages we could do the work of *dawah*, or conveying the message of God, on a very limited scale at a local level. However, today due to the developments in print and electronic communications *dawah* can be performed at a global level. Similarly, earlier while travelling one was hindered in one's journey due to unavoidable obstacles, such as mountains, jungles and oceans. But in today's age aeroplanes have the potential to rise above all obstacles and have made travel swift and convenient.

In the age of kingship, a common man had very few opportunities before him. But today democracy has drastically limited the political power of the ruler, and this phenomenon has opened up great scopes for everyone in a great number of fields. Likewise, the previous age was marked by religious persecution, but today every person enjoys unlimited religious freedom.

The above changes in modern times have rendered violence totally futile. Advances in the present age have made it possible to achieve by peaceful means what could previously be gained only by violent means. Earlier every expansion led to confrontation because it involved encroaching on the domain of others, but now such new ways of development have been discovered that great expansion is possible without the slightest need to resort to confrontation.

It is a fact that man, by nature, is ambitious. Formerly, in order to fulfil his ambitions, he used try either to conquer nations or occupy more land by engaging in one battle after another. But now none of these courses need to be resorted to. Today, technology has become an alternative to such action, as every kind of development and progress can be had without fighting or violence. Indeed, modern technology has opened the doors to peace.

The modern age is one of technology. Those who continue to fight in this age give proof of the fact that they are unaware of the opportunities presented by the new age. They want to continue to live in this age of peace with the outdated mindset of the age of war.

Those Muslims who are fighting to achieve political goals are perhaps unaware that by utilizing the resources of modern technology, they can attain all their goals peacefully.

The European colonial period lasted from the sixteenth to the mid-twentieth century. The basic purpose of colonialism was to secure a global market for the produce of the colonizing nations. At that time, this was possible only by gaining political power over a country. Therefore, colonialism in practice turned into "political colonialism". However, in the present age the industrial nations are fulfilling the same purpose on an even larger scale without having to wage either military or political battles. This change has become possible only through modern technology.

Those Muslims who are fighting to achieve political goals are perhaps unaware that by utilizing the resources of modern technology, they can attain all their goals peacefully. The violent method, on the contrary, can only cause loss of life and property.

Living in a New Age

❦

The problems faced by the Muslim community in the present age have, directly or indirectly, only one cause—that is, unawareness of the advantages of the present age.

The modern age is, in every respect, a new age. If the previous age was a traditional one, the modern age is non-traditional. However, Muslims of the present times are not cognizant of this fact. This is why their planning, done along traditional lines, proves to be fruitless. In other words, the case of present-day Muslims is one of anachronism, that is, living in the present age while still clinging to the mindset of the previous age. Any kind of effort towards the revival of Muslims can be successful only if it effects a change in their way of thinking. It must make them emerge from the past and lead their lives in the present.

During the Italo-Turkish war of 1911-12, Libyan fighters famously used this slogan:

Mutu al-yawm aizza qabla an tamutu ghadan azilla

(Die a respected death today, before you have to die a disrespected death tomorrow)

The banner on which this slogan is imprinted, and which I have personally seen, is still on display in the museum in Tripoli. This slogan may express exactly how present-day Muslims feel, but it goes against the creation plan of God. The right slogan should be: 'Life is a divine gift. It should be utilized for a creative purpose.'

Every human being having been endowed with unique

qualities, it is against the creation plan of the Creator for a man just to fight and get himself killed. Every human being must rather live and make a healthy use of his abilities. All the progress seen in the world was not achieved by those who fought and were killed: it was achieved by those who made good use of the life given to them by the Creator. Had people all over the world engaged in warfare, there would have been no developments in human life; even the modern-day resources which are made use of by militants today would not have come into existence.

Every human being having been endowed with unique qualities, it is against the creation plan of the Creator for a man just to fight and get himself killed.

Even today, innumerable Muslims are influenced by the kind of thinking which inspired the Libyan fighters. Indeed, Muslim violence in the present age stems from this turn of mind. The Muslim groups that perpetrate terror are very well aware that the other side is so strong that their violence cannot seriously affect it in any way. Yet, they continue to engage in acts of violence. The motivation behind this violence is that Muslims falsely believe that if they indulge in violence in the name of jihad, and in the process get killed by their enemies, they will become martyrs and be led straight to heaven.

This is a false belief. No person or group wants to kill Muslims. Rather, Muslims have themselves developed the theory that there is a conspiracy to harm or kill them. This unnatural and unfounded fear causes them to engage in violence, the result of which is but a further deterioration in their own situation. All such cases are instances of attacks being carried out by Muslims causing others to retaliate.

The well-known Syrian poet Khairuddin al-Zirikli (d. 1976)

prepared a multi-volume compendium of famous Muslim personalities of the past, titled *al-A'lām*. He imagined that Muslims could experience a new revival if such great men could be born again. In a couplet of his poem, he expresses this sentiment thus:

Hati salahaddin thaniyatan fina

Jaddidi hittin aw shibh hittina

(Bring back Salahuddin in our midst

Let there be a revival of the Battle of Hattin or battles of similar vigour)

These lines of al-Zirikli reflect the general thinking of Muslims today. Muslim literature chronicles the victories of Salahuddin Ayyubi and Muslim war commanders of earlier Islamic history in great detail and at great length, all of which leads Muslims to think that if a man like Salahuddin were to be born again, he would bring them the kind of victory which was achieved in the twelfth century.

This kind of thinking is the result of a lack of precise knowledge about the present times. Muslims are unaware of the fact that a victory such as Salahuddin's in the twelfth century is simply not possible today. In the present day many leaders, the like of Salahuddin, have been born among Muslims—such as Yasser Arafat, Sayyid Qutb and other *mujahid* leaders— yet, they have not been able to make any notable headway in furthering Muslim affairs. Yearning for the return of Salahuddin is the result of a regrettable unawareness of the realities of the modern age. Muslims need to bear in mind that in the present age, power and strength are determined not by fighting but through advances in science and technology. In this day and age, giving encouragement to the latter factors is the surest way to success.

It is due to the Muslims' failure to take into account the compulsions of the age in their planning that their endeavours by and large have gone awry.

Why are the Youth Joining Terrorist Groups?

⟨❦⟩

*I*n present times Muslim youths are joining terrorist groups in large numbers. This is taken to be an inexplicable phenomenon. Nevertheless, this, based on my experience, can be explained in understandable terms.

The truth is that in their youth, people are very energetic. They want to do something revolutionary and dedicate themselves to a great goal. In order to satisfy this desire, my colleagues and I have adopted a method that is highly workable.

Sensing people's enthusiasm for positive activism, we have planned a project, which is global in its reach and, at the same time, is completely peace-oriented. What it involves is the distribution of translations of the Quran and its supporting literature to all the nations of the world.

To get this project under way, we have decided to prepare translations of the Quran in all the major languages of the world. At present we have published translations in ten languages. When we launched this project, young people, both Muslim and non-Muslim, joined in the work with great enthusiasm. They began to make programmes on their own to take the translations of the Quran to people in different places.

Since, for some reason, the Quran is in the news these days, people show a certain readiness to accept copies of the Quran when it is presented to them in their own languages. This overwhelming response gives a further boost to those who have become part of our project.

At an international conference held in Abu Dhabi under the aegis of the Forum for Promoting Peace in Muslim Societies, from April 28 – 30, 2015, I delivered an address in which I made the point that if we want to change the minds of the Muslim youth, we shall have to give them a peaceful alternative. The best alternative is the global distribution of the Quran.

This goal for Muslims was set by the Prophet of Islam himself in the seventh century, as according to a tradition, he said that in future the word of God would reach every individual and every household of the globe.[1] At that time, this saying did not go beyond being a prediction. But, today modern technology and means of communication have made it possible to fulfil this prediction to the ultimate degree. Furthermore, in present times news of "Islamic violence" finds a place daily in the world media.

Young Muslims have to arise and disseminate the message of the Quran worldwide. This mission is a billion times more attractive for Muslim youths than terrorism.

This situation has led to the Quran becoming a subject of discussion and has increased people's curiosity about the message of the Quran. People are eager to study it. Today we would do well to give Muslim youths the goal of conveying the Quran to those who are keen to know about it.

Young Muslims have to arise and disseminate the message of the Quran worldwide. This mission is a billion times more attractive for Muslim youths than terrorism. The only problem is that Muslim youths have not been made aware of this mission. If they have the importance of this task explained to them in a language which they understand, they will certainly give up violence and rally to the mission of the global dissemination of the Quran.

Recently research was conducted on the subject of terrorism, the findings of which are totally relevant to the present theme. Political scientist V.P. Fortna from Columbia University in her paper on terrorism observes,

'Terror is a cheap way to inflict pain on the other side.'[2]

The present terrorist culture is a result of nurturing anger. What are terrorists doing but hurling their inner negative bombs at their supposed enemies? They should have it explained to them that they have in their possession a more powerful weapon—the Quran, which is like a positive bomb, something which is a billion times more effective than the violent bomb to which they have recourse. This would certainly go a long way towards making these people give up violence in favour of peace.

The above reality has actually been experienced in history. In the early period of Islam, the Arab people were tribal in their culture. They had adopted the culture of the sword— hurling their weapons at their rivals. At that time they were given the Quran which proved to be a positive alternative for them. The ideology of the Quran made the Arabs 'a nursery of (peaceful) heroes.'[3] These early Muslims went beyond the borders of Arabia with the Quran and spread their Quranic mission throughout the world.

The British anthropologist Sir Arthur Keith wrote a book *A New Theory of Evolution* (1948), in which, referring to the ancient history of Egypt, he observes how Islam spread to Egypt during the period of the Caliphate. He says:

'Egyptians were conquered not by the sword, but by the Koran.'[4]

If they were made to realize that the Quran could be an alternative for them, the same history could be repeated with the young Muslims of the present day and the world would see that the violent activists of the past were now turning into the peace-loving heroes of today.

Peace through Education

❦

*L*eo Tolstoy, (1828 – 1910) the Russian novelist, regarded as one of the greatest writers of all time, wrote a short story titled *Wisdom of Children*, first published in 1885.

Tolstoy, referring to an incident in the story, observes that he once watched some children playing together. What was significant about their play was that they would enter into a heated exchange, but their quarrelling would not result in hatred and confrontation. Very soon they would start playing once again as usual.

Tolstoy concludes that this is nature's model for peaceful living. Differences do arise between people but they should not go beyond verbal exchanges. Differences should not lead to hatred, violence, and finally culminate in war. Tolstoy's novel is based on this model of nature.

It is true that nature's model is the same as we find in the life of children. Children are in their formative age, so their egos have yet to develop. They are in the pre-ego stage of life. But when these very children grow up and form part of society, they do not behave in the same manner. All the problems of the world are phenomena of grown-up children. When they grow up, these same children become egoists. This being so, how can the model provided by the ego-less apply to the egoist? During childhood, human beings are governed by their inner nature. But when they grow up and reach the age of maturity, they are governed by their conscious minds. Now their inner nature has a limited role to play. What is needed at this stage is to develop the thinking of adults in such a way that they are enabled to behave in the same manner as they did earlier, in childhood—but consciously, and by using their will power.

Tolstoy and others have written numerous works of fiction. But fiction can only be a source of entertainment and not a tool for the conscious training of the human mind. For the conscious training of readers, it is necessary to write such books as will address their reason and logic. That is, such books have to be based on historical facts, with reference to scientific knowledge, and must give examples of the experiences of real life non-fictitious personalities.

Building a peaceful society requires the re-engineering of the mind. This task can be carried out only through education—more through informal education than formal education.

Fiction caters to a person's sense of enjoyment; it does not address his reason. That is why when we say something through the medium of fiction, it yields no fruitful result; it fails to bring about any actual change in a person's life.

Man's greatest faculty is his ability to think rationally. It is said that man is a thinking animal. Reading fiction can be a source of enjoyment, but if we want to bring about a revolution in a person's life, we shall have to state our facts on the basis of established knowledge and rational analysis. This is the only way to bring about a revolution in a person's thinking. Nothing less than an intellectual revolution can effect any real beneficial change in human life.

Building a peaceful society requires the re-engineering of the mind. This task can be carried out only through education— more through informal education than formal education. By informal education, I mean gaining knowledge through the media, literature, seminars and conferences, dialogue and discussion, and so on.

Here, I am not just theorizing about peace: I have experimented with it in practice. The venue of this experiment was Kashmir. I have been working towards inculcating peaceful thinking among Kashmiris since 1968, and I am still continuing with my efforts. There has been a sea-change as a result of this movement, and now, in almost every house in Kashmir the peace-promoting literature of our mission is read.

In 2011 we organized a meeting of those Kashmiris who are acquainted with our ideas. On this occasion, someone representing a group of Kashmiris said in the course of conversation: 'We have travelled a long way from October 1989 to October 2011. Formerly, we used to throw stones at the Indian army. Now, we present them with literature about peace.'

Kashmir, which after 1947 was continually engaged in militancy, has now almost become a peaceful state. If there is any news of attack or violence from Kashmir, it is not due to the local Kashmiris, but is the result rather of a proxy war conducted from outside.

The above example of bringing about 'Peace through Education' can be experienced everywhere. The most effective way of bringing about peace is only one—and that is, to educate people's minds along peaceful lines.

The best way to bring about change in society is through education. In the pre-printing press age books were not available. So it was not possible to educate people on a large scale—war is a remnant of that ancient age. In those times people tried to bring about change through force, and this led to war.

Now we are living in the age of printing press in which books exist in abundance. It is therefore possible to bring about a change in society through mass education. Those who are engaged in war for the sake of reform only show that they are unaware of this fact. If they realized this, they would throw away their guns and concentrate on education.

Chapter Six
Peace in the Muslim World

Peace of Mind is Most Important

⌒⫘⌒

The mind is the greatest faculty of man and peace is the most favourable environment in which the mind can function to its full capacity.

The mind is the greatest blessing of the Creator. All the great achievements of the world have been as a result of the functioning of the mind. But it requires peace to function smoothly, as without peace one cannot proceed normally.

The Roman Empire ruled the greater portion of Europe and Africa for about 2,000 years. However, there was no scientific development during this long period. Historians generally attribute this phenomenon to the lack of freedom of thought under the Roman rule. Anyone who expressed dissent from the view of the king was put to death. The watchword of this period was that 'the king could do no wrong'. Thus only one person was allowed to think freely and the thinking process of all others was severely constrained. This atmosphere naturally led to intellectual stagnation.

The French Revolution of 1789, in putting an end to the hereditary monarchical system of governance, marked the dawn of a new democratic era in the world. The democratic culture gave every person the freedom to think. If earlier only the king could think, now every individual person was free to think. In this way the thinking process was increased by a billion times over. This intellectual revolution meant that scientists were now intellectually unfettered and had every opportunity to think freely and make new discoveries.

For example, it was due to scientific research that the means of communication, which had been hidden in nature in the form of potential, became a concrete reality. Indeed, according to God's creation plan, everything in this world has always been in its potential form—including all the amenities of the modern age.

The human mind has great potential, but it can only work in a peaceful atmosphere. In the absence of a peaceful environment for work, the mind's capabilities will remain unutilized—the process that unfolds the potential of the mind will be left uninitiated.

But those who are engaged in militancy are running counter to this creation plan of God and in doing so, they are destroying peace. According to the divine scheme of things, it is essential that there should be complete peace in the world so that people may have total freedom to think and work undisturbed. That is the only way in which they can convert the potential of the world into actuality. When a terrorist kills a person, he, in actual fact, kills a mind. If he kills a group of people, he kills a large number of minds. Given this situation, if certain people engage in militancy in the name of a self-styled goal, they are undoubtedly indulging in an act which is entirely undesirable, because in doing so, they are jeopardizing the Creator's scheme of things.

The human mind has great potential, but it can only work in a peaceful atmosphere. In the absence of a peaceful environment for work, the mind's capabilities will remain unutilized—the process that unfolds the potential of the mind will be left uninitiated. In such a situation, those who perpetrate violence are indulging in an act that goes against nature.

Experience also confirms the above fact. Since the time Muslims have taken to violence in the present age, no scientific development has taken place in the Muslim world. The entire Muslim community has been reduced to being a taker community – unlike what it was in the past. According to a principle of nature set forth in the Quran, only those who are givers prove to be successful in this world. (13:17)

Those who are engaged in violence in the Muslim community have become a permanent obstacle to the progress of Muslims. Such people should forthwith cease all their violent activities and bury their weapons, so that an atmosphere of peace may prevail in the Muslim world, thus allowing it to emerge once again as a creative community.

In those countries where terrorism exists, the work of education and scientific development comes to a halt. On the contrary, in countries where there is no terrorism, progress goes unabated in every field. This bears out the old adage that peace promotes all kinds of progress, while violence endangers all kinds of constructive activities.

No constructive target can be achieved by fighting. You cannot grow a tree by fighting. You cannot build a planned city by fighting. You cannot bring a developed civilization into existence by fighting. An educated society cannot be produced by fighting. Those who are engaged in fighting clearly demonstrate that they are totally unaware of the realities of life. Trying to achieve a positive target by fighting is a grave misjudgement of both man and the Creator.

The whole universe is one of peace. But this peace is compulsory in the sense that it has been externally imposed. Then God Almighty wanted to create man who could adopt self-imposed peace or have peace by choice. For this purpose, He settled man on the planet earth and promised the greatest reward for those who could stand up to this test. Those who adopt the culture of vioelnce go against the creation plan of God, thus taking the risk of forfeiting the great reward destined for them by God.

The greatest disadvantage of the culture of violence is that those who engage in it begin to live on the defensive—to the extent that they believe that they are living under siege. A mindset of this kind hampers creative thinking and leads to stagnation. This loss is so huge that there is no justification for continuing to perpetrate violence, even for a single moment.

The Unfinished Agenda

❦

*T*he Chief of Army Staff (COAS) of the Pakistan Army, General Raheel Sharif, addressing a conference at the National Defense University in Islamabad, Pakistan on June 3, 2015, said that Pakistan and Kashmir were inseparable, and that Kashmir was "an unfinished agenda of partition."[1]

The above statement of the Pakistani General tells us much about the Muslim mind of the present times. It is symbolic of why Muslims all over the world are engaged in violence, some being actively involved, while others think along those same lines.

Apparently, there are different groups within the Muslim community, but they all have one thing in common, that is, every group has an "unfinished agenda" which it is actively engaged in trying to achieve. The motivation to strive for this task begins first at the level of the mind, then is soon verbalized in the form of complaints and protests. Finally, it takes the form of violence.

What is this unfinished agenda? For some Muslims it is the unfinished agenda of Pakistan, for others it is the unfinished agenda of Palestine, for yet others it is the unfinished agenda of the Khilafat and, for yet others, it is the unfinished agenda of the Shariah. These are the unfinished agendas for which Muslims of the present times are fighting against supposed enemies. Yet, even after a long passage of time, none of these groups has been successful in achieving its declared goal.

Why has there been this failure? A verse from the Quran throws light on this matter. It says:

'You will overcome them if you are indeed believers.' (3:139)

There are many such verses in the Quran which tell us that success in this world is for one who follows the law of nature set by the Creator. Those who go against the law of nature can never be successful in their endeavours. The law of nature applies to everyone—be it Muslims or any other group.

According to the law of nature, a universal principle is that, in this world, political power cannot be the monopoly of any particular group – it will sometimes be in the hands of one group and, at other times, in the hands of some other group. This principle is stated more than once in the Quran. For example, at one place the Quran says:

'Lord, sovereign of all sovereignty. You bestow sovereignty on whom You will and take it away from whom You please.' (3:26)

According to this principle, not being able to achieve one's goal, in spite of resorting to war, shows that one has been engaged in a wrong war—trying to achieve something which, according to divine law, was impossible to achieve. In such a situation, beginning a war may be permissible for a group, but continuing with war is not at all justifiable.

It is possible for a group to wage war because of having made a wrong assessment of the situation. But when it comes to know that, despite all the wastage of life and property, it is failing to be successful in the path it has adopted, it should immediately abandon this path and follow the right path. In this matter, a wrong beginning can be forgiven, but not subsequently opting for the right goal is quite unforgiveable.

These days various groups among Muslims are fighting for the fulfilment of an unfinished agenda. But events show that all these groups are facing complete failure in achieving their goals. Therefore, the time has come for every group to opt for the right path. It has become necessary for every group to instantly put a stop to its present fighting and to discover, by studying the Quran and the Hadith, to what work it should devote itself.

These days various groups among Muslims are fighting for the fulfilment of an unfinished agenda. But events show that all these groups are facing complete failure in achieving their goals.

Violence is absolutely not an option for Muslims, nor should struggling to achieve political gain be their goal. Muslims have only one choice before them, that is, to engage in peaceful *dawah* work.

A study of the Quran shows that it has been revealed for all mankind. (25:1) Therefore, the greatest unfinished agenda of the Muslim community is only one – and that is the universal dissemination of Quranic teachings.

Muslims need to consider their lack of success in other fields as a divine sign. They must realize that God is not pleased with their present activities. God wants them to work for the right unfinished agenda. If they do this, they will certainly receive God's help. As the Quran says:

'God will surely help him who helps His cause—God is indeed powerful and mighty.' (22:40)

God is waiting to extend His help to those who devote themselves to the right task, that is, peaceful *dawah* work.

De Gaulleism Shows the Way

———✳———

When European colonialism began to extend in all directions in the sixteenth century, the British came to the countries of Asia, while the French made inroads deep into African countries. In 1830 the French seized Algiers, thus beginning the colonization of French North Africa. The French established a large number of colonies in Africa from the seventeenth century onwards and slowly their rule came to extend over about fifteen countries.

This kind of French expansion was bound to produce keen political resentment among the African people. As a result, many freedom movements were initiated in Africa to free it from foreign rule. The French had over and over again to deploy its armies in Africa to bring these resistance movements under control. The military budget spent in maintaining the colonies became unbearable for France, and consequently, its progress and development in other areas were seriously affected. Thus, France lagged behind other nations in the nuclear race.

When Charles De Gaulle became the President of France in 1958, the deterioration of the economic situation had reached alarming levels. De Gaulle's concern was not to maintain the national pride of France, but rather to give new life to the country. When he thought about the issue objectively, he came to the conclusion that, in order to do so, it was imperative to grant independence to the French colonies in Africa. He then entered into negotiations with the African leaders and, within a short period, he had granted freedom to the African countries under French rule.

This was a radical step, and De Gaulle had to pay a heavy price for it: he resigned from the post of president in 1969 as an unpopular leader of France and his death was marked as a non-event.

However, it was because of De Gaulle's policies that France started to develop rapidly and now has the first position in Europe in the field of nuclear science.

Present-day Muslim leaders ought to take a lesson from the above example. Their leadership, instead of bringing any positive gain, has only led to losses for Muslims. In such a situation, leaders who are spearheading the present-day militancy should bring about a drastic change in their policies. They should abandon violence and adopt a peaceful course of action.

Their own leadership may suffer a setback because of such a radical policy, but as far as the Muslim community as a whole is concerned, it will surely begin to make progress along constructive lines. From being a backward community, it will begin its journey towards becoming a progressive community.

The greatest positive aspect of this development would be that the image of Islam – in the eyes of people of the world – would undergo a great change for the better. Because of the continuing Muslim militancy all these years, it has come to be generally believed that Islam is a religion of violence. But if Muslims adopted the peaceful method, Islam would be known as a peaceful religion, which enjoined its followers to work and live peacefully. Indeed, giving a correct picture of Islam is undoubtedly the greatest need of today.

What Charles De Gaulle did was not the personal policy of one individual; it was rather based on the law of nature. This is the policy which is known in common usage as the U-turn policy, that is, a complete reversal of direction.

It is said that to err is human. Any individual or nation can make mistakes. But when one's actions do not produce the required result, one should be ready to immediately revise one's policies and promptly take a U-turn. After all, making mistakes is not irremediable. And often all it takes to save the day is a reversal of policy.

In this day and age, certain Muslim leaders have had recourse to violent activism. Although this course has not been adopted by all leaders but only by some leaders, because of the circumstances of the present age, it has won the support of an overwhelming majority of Muslims. However, experience has shown that this was not the right option, as it has not yielded the desired result. Given this state of affairs, Muslims would be well advised to adopt a 'Better late than never' attitude and to thoroughly revise their policies.

It is said that to err is human. Any individual or nation can make mistakes. But when one's actions do not produce the required result, one should be ready to immediately revise one's policies and promptly take a U-turn.

De Gaulleism is not just a principle adopted by a French general, but is rather a policy which is in line with the universal law of nature. The law of nature says that if results show that one's advance is not working, then one should be ready to adopt the strategy of retreat. In many situations, retreating can also be a way of moving forward.

Low Profile, High Profile

Jamal ad-Din al-Afghani (1839 – 1897) was the most prominent political leader of his time. Due to his excellent qualities, he was offered high positions in several Muslim countries, such as Afghanistan, Iran, Egypt and Turkey. But because of his negative activities he ultimately became unwanted everywhere. He could not achieve his goal and died in frustration, before he was sixty.

Al-Afghani, along with his disciple Muhammad Abduh (1849 – 1905), made Paris the centre of his activities. In 1884 he began publishing a newspaper entitled *al-Urwah al-Wuthqa* (The Indissoluble Link) from Paris. But, because of his political extremism, Muhammad Abduh could not see eye to eye with him. In Paris he told al-Afghani that they were wasting their time in political activities. They should instead establish an educational institution to peacefully educate the Muslim youth. Al-Afghani disliked the proposal and replied: *Innama anta muthabbit* ('You are saying something discouraging'). Thereafter, Abduh terminated his association with al-Afghani and left Paris for Egypt.

Muhammad Abduh had proposed a low-profile way of working, but al-Afghani considered the high-profile way of working to be the right way. Political struggle was for him a high-profile endeavour and educating people was a low-profile project. In the latter case, one makes one's plans on the basis of realities. This means placing oneself in a position of low visibility; as proceeding in this way draws little public attention, people do not regard this as a great task. On the contrary, in the high-profile way of working, a person makes big plans and speaks in a grandiloquent manner, and this increases his visibility. However, in terms of results, working in a low-profile manner bears fruit, whereas the high-profile way of working does not. In the former case, one remains steadfast to the peaceful course, whereas in the latter case, one very soon becomes embroiled in confrontation and violence.

The peaceful method develops modesty. Contrary to this, one who adopts the violent method very soon becomes arrogant.

The greatest assets to humanity are those who are born with superior qualities such as exceptional brilliance and great firmness and resolve. But it has been the sad experience of history that people with such qualities all too often become the victims of misadventure. This is because they are not ready to undertake anything less than a high-profile enterprise. Therefore, they engage in unrealistic planning for the task in hand, and the result is that they generally fail in life. Neither are they able to do anything of significance for themselves, nor can they enhance the lives of others.

The peaceful method develops modesty. Contrary to this, one who adopts the violent method very soon becomes arrogant. The peaceful method develops one's personality in a constructive way and it is the only method that yields a positive result. The violent method, in contrast, ruins a person's personality and destroys the resources at hand.

The low-profile way leads one to success whereas the high-profile way leads to further deterioration of the situation. The reason is that working in a low-profile way is in accordance with the law of nature. And, in this world success is only for those who follow the law of nature.

Take the example of a tree. A tree begins from a small seed. The seed starts growing and after a period of about twenty to thirty years it becomes a fully-grown tree. The growth of the tree takes place gradually. This gradual way of growth is analogous to working in low-profile. If the tree went against this law of nature, it would never fully mature as a tree. Similarly, if a person did not follow the law of nature in life, he would never achieve any success in this world.

The truth is that man has to perform his activities within a society or a social system. Therefore, it is essential for him to take into consideration the factors that lie outside himself. In doing so, he will automatically follow the low-profile way of proceeding. On the other hand, one who lives within and for himself and does not take into account external factors is doomed to failure. This is because attaining success is like the functioning of a cog-wheel. When two cogs work in perfect conjunction with each other, the machine will run efficiently. But if either of the two cogs becomes jammed and fails to move, the machine will cease functioning altogether.

This is the secret of success in life. Those who are ignorant of this principle are the ones who become violent. Taking to violence is only on account of a lack of awareness. If one can shake oneself out of one's unawareness, one will never opt for the violent course of action.

The Road to Peace

~~❦~~

*A*ll things in the universe are entirely interdependent. Things that are interdependent are related to one another in such a close way that each one needs the other in order to exist. The universal law governing this inter-relatedness is also generally applicable to human society, in the sense that, in the human world, great things can happen when each individual plays his own role without interfering in the sphere of others.

At present we see Muslim militancy almost everywhere. And Muslim countries are no exception. When Muslim countries have Muslim rule and Muslim administration, why is militancy also in evidence there? It is because Muslims in these countries are not following the above universal principle.

To illustrate this, I would like to give two examples from the Muslim world.

In Egypt, King Farouk's rule ended in 1952. Then Gamal Abdel Nasser became president. At that time the Muslim Brotherhood took on the role of the opposition to the government. There was a power struggle between these two factions. To settle the matter, the then president Gamal Abdel Nasser, made a good offer to the Muslim Brotherhood. But Sayyid Qutb, the leader of the Muslim Brotherhood, refused the offer. This fact has been mentioned in *The Lives of the Two Revivers – Hasan al-Banna and Syed Qutb*:

'Nasser...tried to persuade Qutb by offering him any position he wanted in Egypt except its Kingship, saying: "We will give you whatever position you want in the government, whether it's the Ministry of Education, Ministry of Arts, etc." Qutb refused every offer.'[1]

Sayyid Qutb was a very important leader of the Arab world and the acceptance of any one of the above proposals would have opened up great opportunities for him. In ancient Egypt, the Prophet Joseph was likewise offered a post in the department of agriculture by the then reigning king. Now, in the same country, Sayyid Qutb was offered the position of head of the department of education by the contemporary government. It would have been highly advisable for Sayyid Qutb to accept the offer and then make plans to educate his people. Had he done so, he would have been very well placed to have an effective influence on a whole new generation in Egypt. In this way, he would have been better able as an educator to bring the Islam he wanted into his country than in the position of an administrator.

The same happened in Pakistan. When General Ayub Khan became the president of Pakistan in 1958, Sayyid Abul Ala Maududi and his party were active in the name of the 'Islamization of Pakistan'. At that time the same series of events took place in Pakistan as in Egypt.

In *The Vanguard of the Islamic Revolution: The Jama'at-i Islami of Pakistan,* Seyyed Vali Reza Nasr writes:

'During a trip to Lahore in 1962 he [General Ayub Khan] invited Mawdudi to the governor's mansion and suggested that he leave politics to the politicians and dedicate himself to religious studies instead. For encouragement he offered Mawdudi the post of vice-chancellor of the Bhawalpur Islamic University. In no mood to be appeased, Mawdudi rejected both the offer and the counsel.'[2]

This offer by Ayub Khan was a golden chance for Sayyid Abul Ala Maududi. By accepting this offer, he would have been able to organize education throughout the whole of Pakistan and thus prepare the minds of a whole new generation, which in turn would have been greatly helpful to him in reforming Pakistan. However, he turned down the offer and a great opportunity was missed.

The grave issue facing the Muslim community today is that they have been left behind in the international race of education. The responsibility for this backwardness rests entirely on the present-day Muslim leaders, who have been unable to recognize the opportunities on offer and have failed to avail of them by wise planning.

Why have Muslims become involved in the violent culture of the present age? There is just one reason for this: Muslims' backwardness in the field of modern education. Because of educational backwardness, they have failed to discover the nature of the modern age.

The grave issue facing the Muslim community today is that they have been left behind in the international race of education. The responsibility for this backwardness rests entirely on the present-day Muslim leaders, who have been unable to recognize the opportunities on offer and have failed to avail of them by wise planning.

The modern age was a supporting factor for Islam, but because of their educational backwardness Muslims have come to regard it as inimical to Islam. This is the basic reason why Muslims have failed to engage in peaceful planning for their revival, and have become unwisely enmeshed in the culture of violence. It is only when they fully realize this fact that there can be a new future for Muslims.

The Crusades as Trendsetter

❧

*T*he Crusades were one of the longest wars in history, beginning from 1095 and continuing intermittently for two hundred years and ending only in 1291.

In these wars, on the one side, all the Muslim rulers were involved. On the other side were the Christian nations of Europe; almost all the Christian rulers of that time participated in them. After bloody battles spanning two hundred years, the result was a glorious victory for the Muslims and a humiliating defeat for the Christians.

In the fourteenth century AD, the state of affairs that prevailed was that, on the one hand, the Muslim nations of Asia and Africa had a great victory to celebrate, while, on the other hand, the Christian nations of Europe were left with nothing but a sense of defeat. Today, the situation is totally different. The Muslims of the present times are suffering from a defeatist mentality. On the contrary, the Christian nations of Europe, including America, have established their supremacy over Muslim nations.

Why is there this strange difference between the two? The reason is that the Crusades became a trendsetter for the two nations, although in two different ways. The Muslims came to believe that war was the greatest means of achieving success, whereas the Christian nations—as a matter of compulsion—developed a different way of thinking, which was that since they could not achieve success on the battlefield, they should begin to devote their energies to peaceful fields. The Christians for their part called these efforts 'Spiritual Crusades'. I would say rather that a better term would be 'Peaceful Crusades'. Subsequently, a silent process was gradually set in motion among the Christian nations based on constructive activities such as study and research. All the books available in those times were acquired and translated into European languages. Research was undertaken in many different fields of knowledge, including, most importantly, that of nature.

This process of peaceful research and study, which continued for a long period of time, ushered in the age of the Renaissance in Christian Europe in the fifteenth and sixteenth centuries.

Developments in the sciences and other fields of knowledge continued uninterruptedly until a new world came into existence in the eighteenth and nineteenth centuries—a world which was different in every respect from that of ancient times. It was a high point in the development of western civilization, and its most prominent aspect was that it totally revolutionized the criterion of power for the first time in human history. In ancient times, war was the criterion that determined power. Now, in this new age, rightly called the 'scientific age', peace had become the source of power. During the Crusades, the Muslim nations achieved victory by winning wars. Now in present times, Christian nations have found a far greater victory by employing a peaceful strategy.

In present times, many Muslims are prone to thinking along the lines of violence. In many places, they are directly or indirectly promoting the culture of guns and bombs. But over a long period, despite the extraordinary sacrifices made by Muslims, they have not been able to achieve any success, whereas the ascendancy of western nations has remained unaffected.

What is the reason for the total failure of the Muslims' violent activities in the present times? There is just one cause and that is their opting for ancient ways and practices in modern times. In other words, opting for the culture of war in an age of peace. Muslims for their part attribute their failure to the conspiracies of western nations. However, in the present day, the reason for the Muslims' failure is to be found within themselves, and that is their total unawareness of the changes brought about in this modern age. This is why they have adopted anachronistic policies.

In the twenty-first century the final hour has come for Muslims to completely abandon the gun culture. They are left with no other option.

In earlier times, military strength was considered the source of power, while today peace itself has become the source of power.

In national life, the greatest importance is given to events which act as trendsetters. The main reason for the Muslims' failure in modern times is that the battle of the Crusades became a trendsetter for them. They came to believe that war was greater than anything else. Since then they have been thinking along these same lines.

On the other hand, for Christian nations, too, the events of the Crusades became a trendsetter, but in a different way. Under the pressure of circumstances, they opted for the path of peace and continued to tread it for a long period of time.

Ultimately, through a long and hard struggle, they changed the very criterion for determining power. In earlier times, military strength was considered the source of power, while today peace itself has become the source of power.

The start of a new era for the Muslims will be possible only when they understand this reality and mould themselves accordingly.

The Vatican as a Principle

⟨~~⟩

*T*he Vatican City is a walled enclave within the city of Rome. With an area of approximately 110 acres, and a population of little more than 800, it is the smallest internationally recognized independent state in the world in terms of both area and population. The independent city-state came into existence in 1929 by the Lateran Treaty between the Holy See and the government of Italy.

For centuries, each succeeding Pope was the uncrowned king of Christian Europe. Today, a palace for the Pope still exists in the city of Rome. But, in later times, great differences arose between the Church and secular people. The Pope ultimately saw that he could not return to the previous position, so he agreed to confine his jurisdiction to the Vatican City, which is recognized by the government of Italy. Eventually, even from this territorially small domain, the Pope continued to hold great religious sway not only over Italy, but also over many other parts of the world.

This history of the Vatican gives us an important principle— if you cannot keep your control over the whole, then agree to restrict yourself to a small part. Muslims who are engaged in infructuous fighting in different countries should take the opportunity to succeed in the same way in other fields—that is, they should be ready to accept a "Vatican".

Now, let us take the case of Saddam Hussein (1937 – 2006). He was the ruler of Iraq for almost twenty-one years. Towards the end of this period, circumstances went against his rule and it became clear that he would not be able to retain his former position. However, he continued to fight unnecessarily until on December 20, 2006 he was executed. Saddam Hussein was an educated person. Had he drawn lessons from history, it would have been possible for him to live in Iraq as in a "Vatican".

At that time, Saddam Hussein owned eight palaces in Iraq. U.N. documents list eight main Saddam Hussein palace compounds containing more than 1,000 buildings – luxury mansions, smaller guest villas, office complexes, warehouses and garages – and covering some 32 square kilometres (7,900 acres) in total.

The area of the Vatican is a mere 110 acres, while the cumulative area of Saddam Hussein's eight palaces was 7,900 acres. This story shows that it could have been possible for Saddam Hussein to establish a peaceful kingdom for himself. He could have given up political power and, with his eight palaces, he could have built the largest university of the world. Stanford University, the second largest university in the world at present, has an area of 8,000 acres. Had Saddam Hussein changed his thinking from the political to the peaceful, he could have made a university compound of 7,900 acres. It would have been regarded as one of the biggest educational centres in the world.

Saddam Hussein was obsessed with political power and so he could not understand the importance of the non-political option available to him. This is the case of all Muslim leaders of the present age—they have remained unrealistically obsessed with political power. But political power has limitations, so it has not been possible for them to achieve their goals through it. When they have not been able to achieve their goals, they have become seriously frustrated, as inevitably happens when human beings go against the law of nature.

Barack Obama entered the White House on January 20, 2009 as the President of the United States of America. He was also elected to serve a second term in November 2012, and was sworn in as president for the second time on January 20, 2013. In the beginning, he was very hopeful of bringing about a change in America under his presidency. But even after serving for two terms, he has not been able to bring about the desired change in his country. He himself admitted this fact on June 18, 2015:

> 'I am frustrated, and you have every right to be frustrated, because Congress doesn't work the way it should. Issues are left untended. Folks are more interested in scoring political points than getting things done – not because any individual member of Congress is a bad person – there are a lot of good, well-meaning, hardworking people out there – but because the incentives that have been built into the system reward short term, reward a polarized politics, reward being simplistic instead of being true, reward division. And as mightily as I have struggled against that, it still is broken.'[1]

This statement has a great lesson for those Muslim activists who are fighting for the same unrealistic goal, that is, to bring about change through political power. Almost all political leaders have been obsessed with political authority. They wanted to acquire political position so that they would be able to bring about change. But history tells us that this is a case of having exaggerated expectations of political power, because when these leaders acquired political authority, they were still unable to bring about any real change.

History shows that no one has been able to bring about change through political activism. According to the law of nature, real change always comes through peaceful struggle in non-political fields.

For his 1991 Gulf war, Saddam Hussein used the word *Umm al-Ma'arik* (Mother of All Battles). But this proved to be a complete failure. Had Saddam Hussein, on the contrary, converted his eight palaces into an educational complex, his peaceful institution would have been alive even today.

History tells us that war is like a rootless tree. A storm can completely uproot it. But a peaceful plan is like a tree which stands upright on its own strong roots and remains unaffected by storms.

A war plan has never been crowned by success in history. However, peaceful plans have always been successful. Those who do not take heed from this experience of history are choosing a course which has neither been successful in the past nor will it ever be so in the future. A war plan is doomed to failure, while a peace plan will certainly bring success.

History tells us that war is like a rootless tree. A storm can completely uproot it. But a peaceful plan is like a tree which stands upright on its own strong roots and remains unaffected by storms.

In the present age the story of all Muslim leaders is like that of Saddam Hussein. Each had the possibility to make a big or small peaceful empire by utilizing whatever resources were available. However, all of them took to violence. In this way they destroyed both themselves and also others.

The time has come to put an end to any violent course of action in the twenty-first century and make new plans to tread the path of peace. The failure of those who choose to take to violence will clearly be attributable to their unwillingness to learn from the past.

Pro-Self Activism, Anti-Self Activism

⟨—※—⟩

The well-known Indian film actress, Priyanka Chopra, said of herself in an interview:

'I have spent all my life being different people so I don't know the real me.'[1]

The present age is one of professionalism. Having a profession means living for others. Therefore, it is true of each person that he lives for others and hardly knows his own self. For example, film actors live for their audiences, businessmen for their customers, lawyers for their clients, politicians for their voters, employees for their company bosses, and so on.

This is why so many people have become non-self actors, that is, they live for others rather than for their own selves. This is surely a great loss for a person, as it is because of this that he almost always remains unaware of himself. He frequently evaluates himself according to others' perceptions and not his own. He is unable to unfold his real potential, and finally dies in this state of unawareness.

The worst case is that of those who are engaged in violence in the present times. Such people are embroiled in the gun and bomb culture. Their case is that of anti-self activists.

Who are the anti-self activists? They are individuals who, in the name of annihilating the enemy, are actually fighting with their own selves—sometimes in the sense of psychological killing and at other times in the sense of physical killing.

If one observes a bird perched on a tree, one will realize that it is a marvel of creation—how intelligently it has been designed by the Creator! The bird's design is completely in accordance with the purpose for which the Creator has given it existence. At all times, the bird remains engaged in trying to fulfil the purpose for which it has been created.

Man's case is a billion times better than that of the bird. In terms of his qualities, man is the best-designed creature of the universe. This aspect of man's personality shows that, having been so well-equipped, he has been created for a higher purpose. This being so, the first task for man is to discover himself and then plan his life accordingly.

Violence, or terrorism, is a negation of God's creation plan for human beings. Indulging in violence means that, instead of properly utilizing one's capabilities, one is doing nothing but getting oneself and others killed. This is why those who adopt the culture of killing are, therefore, said to be involved in 'anti-self activism'.

Violence, or terrorism, is a negation of God's creation plan for human beings. Indulging in violence means that, instead of properly utilizing one's capabilities, one is doing nothing but getting oneself and others killed.

If people are judged on this basis, they can be put into three categories: anti-self activists, non-self activists, and pro-self activists. All persons fall into one or other of these categories.

Terrorists or violent activists fall into the category of anti-self activists, that is, they totally destroy themselves. If a person's friend gifted him a very high quality mobile phone, he would never throw it down, or break it into pieces. No one would want to treat anyone's gifts in this manner. Man's existence is also a gift from the Creator. However, people who are engaged in violent activism are mistreating the Creator's gift to them—they are destroying it instead of using it for the right purpose.

The second category is that of non-self activists. Such people are gravely under-utilizing the potential given to them by their Creator. What they are doing with the gift given to them by the Creator will certainly not be acceptable to Him.

The third case is that of pro-self activists. These people are performing their roles in accordance with the creation plan of the Creator. These are the people who discover themselves and also the world in which they find themselves. Through study and contemplation, they understand the higher realities and then rightly prepare themselves for the purpose for which the Creator has created them.

People who belong to this last category are human beings in the true sense. They make their plans according to the divine scheme of things. They turn their potential into actuality and thus develop themselves. These are the people who qualify themselves according to the right standard set by the Creator. It is people such as these who will be held deserving of the eternal blessings of the life Hereafter. They will grow as trees of God in this world, and in the world Hereafter they will become a beautiful part of the garden of God.

I know of a person who was not able to benefit from a higher education. Therefore, he had to lead his life doing an ordinary job. He would often say with deep regret to a friend of his, 'A person finds life only once.'

This means that life is a very precious gift of the Creator. One should avail of this opportunity, because one will never find it again. After death, one will know only repentance, for death always comes at a point of no return.

This formula or principle applies to those who, to a far greater degree, are involved in violent activities. These people become involved in the culture of violence and, very soon, after killing a number of people, they themselves get killed. Neither have these people themselves availed of the precious opportunities given to them by their Creator, nor have they allowed others to do so.

These people will realize after death that the Creator had given them a golden opportunity in the form of life, but they ended their lives without utilizing it for a higher purpose. So, for all eternity, all they have to look forward to is intense regret.

This is an alarming situation which, once understood to be such, should give a warning to terrorists that they should give up their violent activities at once and engage in peaceful struggle to achieve the higher purpose of life.

The Culture of Terrorism

In previous ages, the culture of terrorism was not widespread and weapons were produced in limited numbers, generally only for monarchs who deployed them in battle. The terror culture is a recent phenomenon: it has become prevalent only since the major upswing in the armaments industry which has turned weapons into readily available commodities.

A recent survey reveals that those who produce deadly weapons for the purpose of killing people experience deep frustration towards the end of their lives. All of them question themselves as to why they engaged in an evil of such proportions. However, they mostly die with this question unanswered.

The Russian arms designer, Mikhail Kalashnikov (1919 – 2013) is a notable example of this. He was best known for having developed the AK-47 assault rifle which was named after him. The Kalashnikov, or AK-47, is one of the world's most familiar and widely used weapons. It is thought that more than 100 million Kalashnikov rifles have been sold worldwide.

Six months before his death, Kalashnikov wrote a letter expressing his anxiety to the leader of the Russian Orthodox Church, Patriarch Kirill. It was published by the Russian daily newspaper *Izvestia* in January 2014. In it, Kalashnikov stated that he was suffering "unbearable spiritual pain" about whether he was responsible for the deaths caused by the weapons he created. 'I keep having the same unsolved question: if my rifle claimed people's lives, then can it be that I... a Christian and an Orthodox believer, was to blame for their deaths?' he asked.

'"The longer I live," he continued, "the more this question drills itself into my brain and the more I wonder why the Lord allowed man to have the devilish desires of envy, greed and aggression."'[1]

This is true also of terrorists. Terrorism begins with hate and ends with repentance. If the suicide bombers were questioned after carrying out their attacks, they would acknowledge that they had committed a very heinous crime. But, unfortunately, we never have the chance to speak to them.

Terrorism always ends in repentance. Terrorism thus has a self-deterrent characteristic—that is, after engaging in a terrorist act the extremist immediately realizes that he had erred.

However, there are some examples of perpetrators of terrorist acts who were not themselves killed and who suffered pangs of remorse. One such example is that of Lee Boyd Malvo (b. 1985), a Jamaican-American convicted murderer who, along with John Allen Muhammad, committed murders in connection with the Beltway sniper attacks in the Washington Metropolitan Area over a three-week period in October 2002. Malvo said in a letter to CNN that he was still 'grappling with shame, guilt, remorse and my own healing, if that will ever be possible.' And a social worker who worked extensively with him said he draws self-portraits that often show him with a tear running down his cheek.[2]

Terrorism always ends in repentance. Terrorism thus has a self-deterrent characteristic—that is, after engaging in a terrorist act the extremist immediately realizes that he had erred. For this reason, terrorism should have come to an end. But not all would-be terrorists think in this way; very few of them desist from violence in order to lead a peaceful life.

Terrorism is still rife because extremists do not reflect on the act that they are about to commit. If they realized beforehand what the result of their violent activities would be, they would never follow this course of action. Rather, they would throw away their guns and bombs and lead a peaceful life.

Terrorism is an unnatural act. Neither reason nor conscience can ever sanction it. But often a person, swept away by emotion, ends up perpetrating terrorist acts. In this regard, education—both formal and informal—would serve as a deterrent factor. Even if there are terrorists who are educated, they are so only in the technical or professional sense; they are deficient in learning in the broader sense of the word. It is better to have recourse to education than to guns if present-day terrorism is to be countered. It is a fact that a "peace bomb", in terms of its result, is more effective than a violent bomb.

A Personal Experience

~~*~~

I am a vegetarian. I am also a born pacifist. My life has been an eventful one and all the events of my life have, directly or indirectly, borne some relation to my peace-loving nature.

Here, I would like to narrate a story which I still vividly remember. It was the year 1984 when I went to visit my elder brother A.A. Khan, who lived in Allahabad, India. His interests were very different from mine. He used to have in his possession two licensed guns and would sometimes go out hunting. When I went to see him, he organized a hunting expedition and asked me to accompany him and his friends. Although hunting was not in accordance with my temperament, I nevertheless agreed to go when my brother insisted.

We reached the outskirts of Allahabad in two cars. The environment there was like that of a jungle with many birds perched on tree tops. My brother wanted to hunt for a certain type of pigeon which was called *kahlak* in the local language. While he and his companions went off hunting, I stood to one side as an unwilling onlooker.

Then my brother approached, handed me a loaded 12-bore gun and urged me to aim for a *kahlak* with it. So I stood underneath a tree and sighted a *kahlak* perched on one of the branches. I placed the gun on my shoulder and tried to take aim. When the bird came within range and I had to simply press the trigger, a question suddenly came to my mind: why was I killing the bird? My conscience answered that I had no right to kill the bird. When I realized this, I could not press the trigger and returned the gun to my brother. I felt so disconcerted that I immediately left the place and travelled back alone to the Allahabad city by bus.

The culture of violence is apparently directed against someone else. But in fact it is against reality. When a violent person tries to kill another, he is not aware of the grave reality, that is, of the Angel of Death standing behind him. When he has killed others, he too, will, sooner or later, come into the grip of the Angel of Death, who will take him to the Lord of the Worlds to be held accountable for his deeds. If a person holding a gun were to remember this reality, he would never – for any reason whatsoever – aim it at anyone or press the trigger. He would only engage in peaceful struggle to achieve the purpose of his life.

Whenever I hear news of terrorism, I always remember the above experience I had at Allahabad. I think that terrorists are also human beings just as I am. They have the same conscience as I have, so why does not their inner voice ask them why they are killing their fellow men? What right do they have to kill a person whom they did not create in the first place? They would not like anybody to kill them, then why perpetrate this crime against others? Are the terrorists made of stone? If the gun I was given to kill the bird fell from my hand, why do the guns not similarly fall from the hands of these terrorists when they are about to kill other people?

This thought troubles me time and again. I find that terrorists have become negative because they base their actions on a one-sided study of events. For example, a news report lists the books that are read by terrorists, most of which are on war.

This is evident from the collection of documents recovered from Osama bin Laden's Abbottabad compound. These included the books which Bin Laden and his people had been reading. Some of them are *America's "War on Terrorism"* by Michel Chossudovsky, *Guerilla Air Defense: Antiaircraft Weapons and Techniques for Guerilla Forces* by James Crabtree,

Obama's Wars by Bob Woodward, *The U.S. and Vietnam 1787-1941* by Robert Hopkins Miller, *Bloodlines of the Illuminati* by Fritz Springmeier.[1]

This shows that the terrorists have become conditioned in negativity towards others. Perhaps they never come into contact with people who could decondition their minds. If the terrorists ever met such people, I am certain that they would rethink their philosophy and abandon their violent culture. Once their conscience became activated, they too would abandon their guns, just as I did.

There are many young people who have read my writings on peace and have been influenced by them. They have then decided to lead a peaceful life.

I have had many such related experiences. For example, in 1993 an extremist group put me on their hit-list. At that time, a young man entered my office one day in New Delhi when I was alone. I surmised that there must be a revolver in his pocket, as his hand never left his pocket. I thought for a moment and then I went up to him, and sitting next to him, I placed my hand on his head and said to him: 'You see, I am like your father. My advice to you is to take admission in a school. I promise you that I will pay for your education till you have completed your studies.' The young man fell silent and then he got up and quietly left with his head bowed.

There are many young people who have read my writings on peace and have been influenced by them. They have then decided to lead a peaceful life.

Terrorists are not basically corrupt individuals. They are rather wrongly conditioned human beings. We should try to alter their thinking by applying reason, and without doubt terrorism will disappear.

Chapter Seven

Islam and Peace

Islam the Religion of Peace

⚜

There are two basic teachings of Islam: monotheism and peace. *Tawhid* (monotheism) is Islam's basic ideology. It is the source of all direct or indirect acts of Islam. Peace is its practical aspect, being at the basis of a normal environment in which Islam's ideological and practical teachings may come into play.

When we study the Quran, we find that the Quran's greatest concern is the world Hereafter and not the present world, because the former is eternal while the latter is only a transient phase. According to the Quranic concept, preparing for this world is a necessity, while preparing for the Hereafter is a goal. As such, the focus of those who come under the influence of Islamic ideology shifts wholly to the Hereafter and Paradise.

Consequently, it is but natural that all those things which ultimately result in war lose in importance, for instance, greed, hatred, rivalries, violence, and so on. In this way, wherever Islamic culture prevails these reasons for war will no longer exist. In their own interest, people will live in society as peaceful citizens.

It is greed for political power which has always been the cause of war throughout history. However, Islam laid down the principle that the system of government would be based on mutual consultation. This command is expressed in these words in the Quran: *Amruhum shura baynahum.* That is,

'Their affairs are settled by mutual consultation.' (42:38)

This means that in Islam, governance is not imposed from outside. Rather, it emerges from within society. It is not a matter of imposition by anyone. This has been expressed in a Hadith in these words:

'As you are, so will be your rulers.'[1]

The reason for wars in the name of political power has always been a person's or group's desire to establish their rule in society by removing their rivals from power. This leads to wars between the two parties. But when the principle adopted is that political rule is not a matter of imposition, but is rather something which emerges from within society, the reasons for war are automatically eliminated.

If anyone has any ideas about the course politics should take, he or she has only one option, and that is, to peacefully disseminate his or her ideas. Instead of attempting to impose one's ideas upon others, one has to wait until society willingly accepts them. The enforcement of political ideas is not an option for anyone.

There are a number of such traditions as enjoin people to totally refrain from confrontation with their rulers. If they have any complaints against their rulers, they should change their field of action. Instead of politics, they should devote their energies to other fields. There are a number of traditions under the heading *Kitab al-Fitan* recorded in books of Hadith. On this subject al-Imam al-Nawawi has thus described the opinion of the ulama:

'Only peaceful advice can be given to the ruler of the time. So far as revolt (*khuruj*) and war (*qital*) against them are concerned, it is unlawful (*haram*) by the consensus of the ulama, even if someone thinks that the ruler is corrupt (*fasiq*) and oppressive (*zalim*).'[2]

This principle does not mean abandoning politics. Rather, it has great wisdom in it. It shows that Islam has enjoined a division of the spheres of activity. If you study the Quran, especially verse 41 of Chapter al-Hajj (The Pilgrimage) and other verses on this subject, you will find that the Quran differentiates between two domains of life: the political and the non-political. The Quran suggests maintaining a division of labour between the two. According to the Quran, the duty of the ruling party is to maintain peace and stability in society, while the duty of reformers is to confine themselves to non-political activities, such as education—both formal and informal, *dawah* work (conveying the message of God to people), inculcating right thinking in people and so on. Thus the two groups can play their roles in building a better society. In this way all kinds of work will be carried on smoothly and there will be no occasion for confrontation. The principle of the division of work obviates the need for confrontation and clash in society. As a result, society is blessed with an ambience of peace, not war.

The truth is that Islam in the full sense is a religion of peace. In no way is it a religion of war. In Islam, peace is the rule and war is only a rare exception.

This and other such teachings which are set forth in the Quran and the Hadith are aimed at putting an end to the prevalence of war and violence in society. In this way a normal and propitious environment is established, in which all kinds of healthy and constructive activities become possible.

The truth is that Islam in the full sense is a religion of peace. In no way is it a religion of war. In Islam, peace is the rule and war is only a rare exception. Moreover, this exception was applicable in previous ages when tribal culture prevailed in the world. Now this is a totally different age. Today we are living in the age of democracy and the United Nations. Therefore, the word 'war' has become an obsolete term in the international dictionary. If any war takes place in the present, it goes against the universal norm.

Interdependence— A Law of Nature

~~❦~~

*A*ccording to the law of nature, human life is based on the principle of interdependence. Disparities are inherent in our social structure, and society can only be cohesive and peaceful if each member accepts these disparities along with the obvious necessity for interdependence. This law of nature is referred to in the Quran in these words:

> 'Is it they who apportion the blessing of your Lord? It is We who distribute among them their livelihood in the life of this world, and raise some of them above others in rank, so that they may take one another into service; and the blessing of your Lord is better than [the wealth] which they amass.' (43:32)

This Quranic verse makes it clear that it has been divinely ordained that there shall be no uniformity among people, but rather disparity. This disparity is based on great wisdom, which is that people should know that, according to the Creator's scheme of things, no individual is self-sufficient in this world; an individual completes himself only by associating with others. In other words, each member of society must accept that interdependence is an ineluctable state of viable societal existence.

It is essential that people should accept disparities as matters of fact. Acknowledgment of this reality will go a long way towards putting an end to social unrest. By accepting that disparity is a positive feature of human life, one has to concede that, according to the creation plan of the Creator, the entire system of the world has to be based on interdependence. Acceptance of this fact will help to eliminate violence from society.

Unwillingness to acknowledge the disparity that is characteristic of human society will result in rivalry between people. In the name of removing disparity from the world, people will engage in confrontation and violence. A never-ending cycle of violence will then come into existence.

If, however, people were to accept disparity as a reality, the culture of cooperation would be promoted in society. Every individual would seek to cooperate with his fellow men and, in this way, a collective culture would be given encouragement. The culture of collective cooperation undoubtedly helps to establish peace in society.

Unwillingness to acknowledge the disparity that is characteristic of human society will result in rivalry between people. In the name of removing disparity from the world, people will engage in confrontation and violence. A never-ending cycle of violence will then come into existence.

Those who are engaged in violence, are not fighting against any person or group, but rather against the very creation plan of the Creator. There are a number of commandments in the Islamic scriptures which forbid violence. The reason is that the culture of violence runs counter to the divine creation plan. According to this plan, if a person or group possesses political power, others should consider this situation as God-given and should not engage in a campaign to unseat those in power.

In other words, the creation plan requires that the status quo should be maintained. The principle of 'status quoism' is the only workable formula for achieving peace in this world. Trying to bring about a change in the status quo leads to conflict, while making plans for one's activities by accepting the existing state of affairs leads to peace.

If a person or group has any complaint or difference of opinion, they should strictly adhere to peaceful negotiation. Trying to bring about change through violence is not an option for anyone. No excuse whatsoever is acceptable in this regard.

Disparity among men and women is not an evil: it is rather a blessing. When people complement each other, it promotes the culture of cooperation, which further leads to the creation of an atmosphere of peace and friendship.

The culture of interdependence promotes all kinds of human values and is, therefore, the best social scheme. Those who have opted for violence are not only destroying social peace, but are also pursuing a target which is unachievable. Interdependence is a law of nature. Accepting the principle of interdependence brings peace to society and opens up all doors to development.

The Greatest Evil of History

~❦~

*W*ar is not a new phenomenon. It has always been a part of human history. In the very first generation of man, fighting broke out between Adam's two sons and, as a result, Abel was killed by his brother Cain. Fighting has continued since then in every group and nation. But we learn from history that every period of conflict has its end. It has always had a limited span. There is no battle which has raged indefinitely; even the First and Second World Wars were fought for limited periods of time.

But the case of the Muslim community appears to be totally different. We learn from history that once a battle is waged in the Muslim *ummah* it never comes to a halt. There is a saying of the Prophet in the nature of a prediction, which has proved to be entirely right. It is as follows:

'When the sword enters the ranks of my *ummah* it will never be taken away.'[1]

In this respect, Muslims have become an exceptional community. A deeper analysis of this matter shows that the reason for this is a justification having been found for violence. That is, violence has been legitimized by religious law. Since, sacred law is unchangeable, the violence which is held justified by it allows no room for revision.

What is this 'justified violence'? It is the perpetration of violence in the name of Islamic jihad. In Muslim history, all battles were fought in the name of jihad. And the traditional concept of Islamic jihad is that success awaits one in either of the two situations: in the case of victory as well as defeat.

If they are victorious, Muslims who engage in jihad gain in worldly terms and in the case of defeat and death, they become martyrs and go straight to Paradise.

Properly speaking, in Islam, jihad in the sense of *qital*, or war, is undertaken only in defence. Since defence is a matter only for the state, it takes place infrequently.

All those Muslim activists who are engaged in war in the name of Islam are "non-state actors". No established Muslim state is involved in this act. The nature of this present violence is in itself un-Islamic. It is an accepted principle of Islam that

'To declare war is the prerogative of an established state.'[2]

According to this principle, all those Muslim *mujahideen* who are engaged in war have no justification to do so in Islam. Such people must unilaterally and unconditionally abandon all their activities and adopt totally peaceful methods.

The fact is that this concept of justified war – actually, a wrongful war – has been developed on the basis of a wrong interpretation of the Islamic scripture, both the Quran and the Hadith.

In present times, in particular, there is no possibility of such war. Now, according to modern universal norms, man has been left no option but that of peace.

The battles waged by Muslims in later times have not been in defence of their country, but—according to their own claim—have been engaged in in order to eradicate tyranny and establish justice. This is without doubt a war of their own innovation. Nowhere in the Quran or the Hadith have Muslims been commanded to resort to war for the purposes of eradicating oppression and establishing justice.

The fact is that this concept of 'justified war' – actually, a wrongful war – has been developed on the basis of a wrong interpretation of the Islamic scripture, both the Quran and the Hadith.

The worst form of this actually unjustified war is that which, in the beginning, is directed against other nations, but, in its second phase, develops into infighting amongst Muslims.

The reason is that when combatants see that they have derived nothing positive from war, they think that there must be some conspiracy against them which explains why their efforts have become futile.

They even come to regard the people of their own community as conspirators, and imply that their failure is due to their machinations, and, this said, they direct their animosity at their own community.

When things come to this pass, the evil goes beyond all limits, that is, Muslims start killing Muslims. The Prophet of Islam had already predicted this evil, which he said would creep into the *ummah*. According to a Hadith, the Prophet observed:

'Do not turn *kafirs* after me, killing one another.'[3]

This prediction of the Prophet has been fulfilled in the twenty-first century. Today we see all over the world that Muslims are killing one another. In most incidents of suicide bombing both the bomber and the bombarded are Muslims.

This phenomenon tells us that, in present times, violence among Muslims is the worst kind of evil. It is a warning to Muslims that if they do not repent and abandon the way of killing and bloodshed, they are taking the risk of being held as *kafirs* in the eyes of God.

This prophetic warning should be enough to make the Muslims of today sincerely repent and altogether give up violence without a moment's delay. They should throw their weapons into the sea and lead their lives as peaceful citizens. There is no other option for these Muslims.

God Calls to the Home of Peace

$\sim$

The following is a verse in the Quran which is of relevance to the present situation of Muslims:

'And God calls to the Home of Peace.' (10:25)

Here, 'Home of Peace' means Paradise, Paradise being the place of ideal peace. God Almighty calls to all mankind: 'If you are desirous of entry into eternal Paradise, you shall have to adopt the culture of peace. You shall have to develop your personality along peaceful lines.'

In another verse the Quran, referring to Paradise, describes its environment thus:

'They will not hear therein any vain or sinful talk, only the words of peace and tranquillity.' (56:25–26)

This is the best description of Paradise. It is an ideal place. It is a perfect society. There will be no nuisance or uncalled for activities there. In Paradise, the culture of peace will prevail in every sense of the term. Implicit in this description of Paradise there is a warning to all: 'O people, if you want to find entry into Paradise, abandon all kinds of violent activities. Adopt the culture of peace. Paradise is a hate-free place. Those who live in hate in this world can never be settled there.'

The Prophet was a peace-loving person in the complete sense of the word. It is a fact that some battles did take place during the lifetime of the Prophet, but all of these were fought in self-defence. One of these was fought at Badr in 624 AD. The traditions tell us that when the battle was taking place, the Prophet Muhammad was sitting some distance away from the battlefield in a makeshift camp. He was seen drawing some lines on the sand. Major Akbar Khan, a writer, making the assumption that his actions must relate to the battle, observed,

'The leader of Islam was making his next war plan.'[1]

This judgment was based only on conjecture, without taking into account the facts. But when we look at other traditions, it becomes clear that what the Prophet was doing at that time was making a plan to establish future peace.[2]

This tradition tells us about the thinking of the Prophet. His mind was not political, but only prophetic. His concern was not to establish his rule in the world but to convey to people a non-political message.

We know this from another Hadith, in which it is said that the Prophet was once sitting among his companions, when the angel Gabriel appeared. At that time an angel descended from the skies. Gabriel told the Prophet:

"'O Muhammad this angel has come down to earth for the first time since it was created.' The angel said to the Prophet: "O Muhammad, God has sent me to you. He has asked me to question you: what do you want to become—a king-prophet or a messenger-prophet?" Gabriel said to the Prophet: "Adopt the way of modesty for the sake of your Lord, O Muhammad." The Prophet answered: "Messenger-prophet.""[3]

This tradition tells us about the thinking of the Prophet. His mind was not political, but only prophetic. His concern was not to establish his rule in the world but to convey to people a non-political message.

Similarly, there is a prayer of the Prophet which says:

'O God, You are peace. Peace comes from You and peace

returns to You. O God, bless us to live in peace. O God, give us entry into the Home of Peace. O God, You are the greatest.'[4]

These words and what actually happened after the battle tell a very different story. In the above war the Prophet had participated out of compulsion, because his opponents had launched an offensive. But later the Prophet continually tried to avoid war, and finally during a negotiation he unilaterally accepted the conditions of his opponents only so that there could be peace between the two parties. In this way, the Peace Treaty of Hudaybiyyah came into being.

The truth is that war is against the creation plan of God. According to God's scheme of things, every person who is born on earth should develop his personality along spiritual lines. He should remove all negativity from within and make himself totally positive in mind. According to the Quran, every person should strive to develop a sublime character. (68:4)

In brief, God's plan is that the process of character building should continue uninterruptedly in the life of every individual. This process can fructify only in an atmosphere of peace, and not of violence and fighting. In such a situation, it is not just to some human being's design that the war-mongers run counter: it is the divine plan with which they are at variance. This is tantamount to jeopardizing God's scheme of things.

Taking the option of war is a crime which God will never forgive. A clear proof of this is that those who have opted for war have not been able to achieve the desired results, even after making great sacrifices over many decades. Indeed, all that they have done is bring ruination to the lives of Muslims as well as to the lives of others.

Managing Human History

We learn from the Quran that one of the laws of history is the law of 'repelling'. It has been mentioned thus in the Quran:

> 'If God were not to repel some people by means of others, the earth would be filled with corruption.' (2:251)

The law of repelling here means that God has granted man total freedom, but at the same time He is constantly watching the human world. While maintaining human freedom, He is constantly managing history. On account of this management of history, man's misuse of freedom does not culminate in any major corruption.

The truth is that the freedom granted to man by the Creator has a special purpose. That is, it is designed for man to develop his personality in this world. This purpose cannot be fulfilled without having freedom. But freedom often leads to the misuse of that very freedom. That is why the Creator is constantly keeping a watch over the evolution of human history, so that the wrong use of freedom never goes to such extremes that the creation plan of the Creator is jeopardized. This was why the Creator put an end to the age of monarchy, through the French Revolution, for the system of monarchy did not allow human freedom.

In 1922 with the establishment of the Communist empire, strict limitations were put on human freedom. This was totally against the creation plan of God. That is why in 1991 the 69-year old Communist empire was dismembered. This did not happen by accident, but was certainly due to the management of history by God.

Now the same process is at work for those who, with self-styled justification, have launched violent movements. It is these kinds of activities which have been characterized as terrorism. This terrorism mostly functions through non-state actors and is totally against the creation plan of God. It is certain that it will have only a limited lifespan.

In my view, this terrorism, whether perpetrated in the name of jihad or in any other name will, without doubt, be extirpated by God. Indeed, we can safely say that the process of extirpation has already started.

The expected outcome of terrorism tells us that probably very soon the post-terrorism age will dawn, and that it will be an age of peace.

In spite of great sacrifices, the terrorist groups have been unsuccessful in achieving their goals. These militant groups have only wrought death and destruction in the world. Consequently, world opinion has turned against them. The terrorists have failed to make any contribution which may be recorded in history in positive terms. This negative result is a clear sign that the Creator has rejected them and that, in Quranic terms, the law of repelling is at work against them. It is almost certain that very soon this terrorism will be rooted out or it will be considerably weakened.

This expected outcome of terrorism tells us that probably very soon the post-terrorism age will dawn, and that it will be an age of peace. Those constructive activities will then be initiated which are desired by the Creator, but which have not as yet materialized due to terrorism.

One of the most important aspects of all activity in the age of peace will be that religion and violence will be practically separated from one another. This separation will undoubtedly usher in a new era of peace for humankind.

The media image of the present world is one fraught with violence. But the situation behind the scenes is quite different—a silent process is going on in the midst of apparently violent activities. This process is taking history from violence towards peace.

According to a report from the Stockholm International Peace Research Institute (SIPRI), there are nine nations which at present possess nuclear weapons. All these countries are facing some problem or the other, but none has used these weapons after the dropping of atomic bombs on Hiroshima and Nagasaki in 1945.

The horrendous outcome of the use of nuclear bombs marked the final stage of violence. When the final form of violence has been used, there are no more commas to violence left. A full-stop is rather put to violence. It is therefore certain that these bombs will never be used again. The utter devastation caused by the use of nuclear bombs in the Second World War sent out a message that the strategy of violence is no longer workable.

There is every sign that human history is marching from violence to peace.

Universal Peace Centre

❦

*A*lfred Nobel (1833 – 1896) who was born in Stockholm, Sweden, worked at his father's arms factory as a young man. Intellectually curious, he went on to experiment with chemistry and explosives, finally developing the use of dynamite. Thanks to his acumen as an industrialist and the patents he took out on explosives, Nobel became a multimillionaire.

In 1864 there was a lethal blast in his nitroglycerine factory, in which his younger brother and several other people were killed. A French newspaper mistakenly thought it had been Alfred Nobel himself who had died and it published his obituary under the title: *The Merchant of Death is Dead*. The obituary said:

'Dr Alfred Nobel, who became rich by finding ways to kill more people faster than ever before, died yesterday.'[1]

When Nobel read this, he was shocked. He began thinking about how to improve his badly damaged image and decided to leave behind his enormous fortune to fund a set of prizes named after him. Thus, in his last will, Nobel bequeathed 94% of his total assets, 31 million Swedish *kronor* (about 186 million US dollars), to establish and endow the five Nobel Prizes. The Nobel Prize organization has come to be known for giving awards to the greatest achievements throughout the world in the field of peace and other disciplines.

Alfred Nobel's plan of image building was a great success. Today the world knows him as a great promoter of peace. The story of how Alfred Nobel invented weapons which he sold to earn money – all of which tarnished his image – is relevant to the Muslims of the present day.

The Muslims of today, for some political reasons, are engaged in the same practice, but with a difference: whereas Alfred Nobel organized the trade of weapons, Muslims organized the culture of violence on the basis of modern arms. If Alfred Nobel was indirectly involved in the killing of human beings, Muslims became directly involved in this killing.

In the case of Alfred Nobel, his personal image was damaged. But in the case of the Muslims, it was far more serious. Muslims having propounded their culture of violence in the name of Islam, and then acted upon it, it was the image of Islam itself which was damaged. This age being the age of the media, the negative news of every instance of violence perpetrated by Muslims was instantly spread all over the globe. Throughout the entire world, the image of Islam became that of a religion of violence.

Alfred Nobel did not waste his time in laying the blame for his infamous reputation at the door of others, but rather took the entire blame upon himself and decided to change his image by making a unique plan for peace.

Now the time has finally come for Muslims to take a similar U-turn without any delay. Muslims must follow the commandment of God expressed in these words:

'Believers, turn to God, every one of you, so that you may prosper.' (24:31)

The best way to initiate an image-building process is that Muslims all over the world must establish a large institution with the name *Universal Peace Centre*. All the Muslim countries, organizations and Muslims with resources should become members of this centre. The *Universal Peace Centre* should be set up with the common support of all Muslims. It should be structured in accordance with international standards and should be completely non-political, non-communal and non-commercial. The sole purpose of this centre should be to promote peace and replace the culture of violence with the culture of peace all over the world.

The Universal Peace Centre should be set up with the common support of all Muslims. It should be structured in accordance with international standards and should be completely non-political, non-communal and non-commercial.

The Muslim community owes a debt to God—that is, Muslims have to spread the word of God to every man and woman on this earth. This task has to be carried out to the fullest extent by peaceful means. The *Universal Peace Centre* will be a means to fulfil this global responsibility of the Muslims. God will surely assist Muslims if they devote themselves to the task of changing the image of Islam—which, at the moment, is that of a religion of violence—to that of a religion of peace.

At present, Muslims are more than one billion in number and are spread out all over the world. All kinds of rich natural resources are available in Muslim countries. The best use of these resources would be to utilize them for the image-building of Islam, and the *Universal Peace Centre* should be designed to fulfil this very purpose.

Notes

Foreword

1. Sahih, Al-Bukhari, Hadith no. 3062.

Chapter I: Peace for the Sake of Peace

On Pacifism

1. International Labour Organization, <http://www.ilo.org/global/about-the-ilo/history/lang--en/index.htm>, [accessed on July 19, 2015].

Peace and Justice

1. International Labour Organization, <http://www.ilo.org/global/about-the-ilo/history/lang--en/index.htm>, [accessed on July 19, 2015].

Chapter II: The Advent of the Age of Peace

The Age of De-monopolization

1. John Frederick West, The Great Intellectual Revolution, New York, The Citadel Press, 1966.

Western Civilization

1. Sahih, Al-Bukhari, Hadith no. 3062.

Making a Friend out of an Enemy

1. The Bible, Matthew 5: 44.

2. "The Search for Adam and Eve," Newsweek, January 11, 1988.

Chapter III: The Non-Confrontational Methods for Peace

The Creation Plan of the Creator

1. Sahih, Al-Muslim, Hadith no. 2593.

The Policy of Mutual Non-interference

1. Ibn Hisham, Sirat Ibn Hisham, Egypt, Mustafa al-Babi al-Halabi & Sons, 1955, Vol. 1, p. 503.

The Save Yourself Formula

1. The Bible, Luke 6: 29.

2. Sahih, Al-Bukhari, Hadith no. 1871.

The Policy of Delinking

1. E.E. Kellet, A Short History of Religions, London, Victor Gollancz Ltd., 1993, p. 334.

The Power of Peace is Greater than the Power of Violence

1. Michael H. Hart, The 100: A Ranking of the Most Influential Persons in History, New York, Citadel Press, 1978, p. 3.

2. Sahih, Al-Bukhari, Hadith no. 3560.

The Examples Set by Two Prophets

1. The Bible, Genesis 41: 40.

Chapter IV: The Experience of History

Living between Idealism and Pragmatism

1. James Jeans, The Mysterious Universe, Cambridge, Cambridge University Press, 1930, p. 3.

Peaceful Planning on the Basis of Realities

1. Rajmohan Gandhi, Eight Lives: A Study of the Hindu-Muslim Encounter, New York, Suny Press, 1986, p. 174.

2. "Musharraf speech highlights, BBC, January 12, 2002," <http://news.bbc.co.uk/2/hi/south_asia/1757251.stm>, [accessed on July 19, 2015].

Violent Activism, Peaceful Activism

1. Edward Gibbon, The History of the Decline and Fall of the Roman Empire, Norwalk, The Easton Press, 1974, Chapter 3, p. 69.

A Prediction that Proved to be True

1. Sakina Yusuf Khan, "US Aggression would be Counter-Productive," The Times of India, New Delhi, September 16, 2001, <http://timesofindia. indiatimes.com/india/US-aggression-would-be-counter-productive/ articleshow/471929455.cms>, [accessed on July 20, 2015].

2. "The British Empire," Caledonian Mercury (15619), 15 October 1821, p. 4.

Maintain the Historical Status Quo

1. Sahih, Al-Bukhari, Hadith no. 126.

Lessons from History

1. John Toland, The Rising Sun: The Decline and Fall of the Japanese Empire, 1936-1945, New York, Random House, 1970, p. 817.

2. Izzuddin ibn al-Athir, Al-Kamil fi al-Tarikh, Beirut, Dar Sadir, 1982, Vol. 12, p. 384.

3. Thomas Walker Arnold, The Preaching of Islam, London, Constable and Co. Ltd., 1913, Chapter: The Spread of Islam among the Mongols and Tartars, pp. 168-192.

4. Phillip K. Hitti, History of the Arabs, London, Palgrave MacMillan, 2002, p. 488.

Chapter V: The Need for a Counter-Ideology

The Case of Present-Day Muslims

1. The Bible, Isaiah 43: 12.

It Requires a Literary Bomb

1. Eugene Lyons, "Milovan Djilas and the Book That Is Shaking the Communist World," Reader's Digest, October 1957.

2. "Battling Islamic State," The Hindu, June 12, 2015, p. 10.

3. Tim Ross, "David Cameron tells teenage jihadists they are 'cannon fodder'", The Telegraph, July 19, 2015, <http://www.telegraph.co.uk/ news/worldnews/islamic-state/11748953/David-Cameron-tells-teenage-jihadists-they-are-cannon-fodder.html>, [accessed on July 21, 2015].

4. UNESCO, <http://www.unesco.org/new/en/unesco/about-us/who-we-are/history/constitution/>, [accessed on July 19, 2015].

The Evil of Selective Information

1. Siobhan Fenton, "Church of England 'one generation away from extinction' after dramatic loss of followers," The Independent, June 1, 2015, <http://www.independent.co.uk/news/uk/church-of-england-one-generation-away-from-extinction-after-dramatic-loss-of-followers-10288179.html>, [accessed on July 19, 2015].

2. "United Airlines faces boycott for 'Islamophobia' at 30,000 feet," The Times of India, New Delhi, May 31, 2015, p. 22.

Suicide Bombing

1. Sahih, Al-Bukhari, Hadith no. 3062.

2. Khalil Gibran, The Prophet, New York, Knopf Doubleday Publishing Group, 1923, Chapter 12.

3. Sahih, Al-Bukhari, Hadith no. 1312.

It All Depends on the Angle of Vision

1. *Leslie Vernick, Lord, I Just Want to Be Happy, Eugene, Harvest House Publishers, 2009, p. 204.*

Why are the Youth Joining Terrorist Groups?

1. Musnad Ahmad, Hadith no. 23814.

2. Virginia Page Fortna, "Do Terrorists Win? Rebels' Use of Terrorism and Civil War Outcomes," International Organization, Vol. 69, Issue 03, Summer 2015, pp. 519-556.

3. Phillip K. Hitti, The Arabs: A Short History, Washington DC, Regnery Publishing, 1996, p. 57.

4. Arthur Keith, A New Theory of Evolution, London, Watts & Co., 1948, p. 303.

Chapter VI: Peace in the Muslim World

The Unfinished Agenda

1. Mateen Haider, "Pakistan and Kashmir are inseparable: General Raheel Sharif," Dawn, June 3, 2015, <www.dawn.com/news/1185928>, [accessed July 19, 2015].

The Road to Peace

1. The Lives of the Two Revivers – Hassan al-Banna and Syed Qutb, <https://archive.org/details/TheLivesOfTheTwoRevivers-HasanAlBannaSyedQutb>, p. 24, [accessed July 19, 2015].

2. Vali Nasr, The Vanguard of the Islamic Revolution: The Jama'at-i Islami of Pakistan, Oakland, University of California Press, 1994, p. 153.

The Vatican as a Principle

1. Chris Cillizza, "Two paragraphs that sum up the Obama presidency," The Washington Post, June 19, 2015, <http://www.washingtonpost.com/blogs/the-fix/wp/2015/06/19/two-paragraphs-that-sum-up-the-frustrations-of-the-obama-presidency/>, [accessed July 19, 2015].

Pro-Self Activism, Anti-Self Activism

1. The Times of India, New Delhi, May 29, 2015, p. 20.

The Culture of Terrorism

1. "Kalashnikov 'feared he was to blame' for AK-47 rifle deaths," BBC News, January 13, 2014, <http://www.bbc.com/news/world-middle-east-25709371>, [accessed on July 19, 2015].

2. Soledad O'Brien, "Sniper says he feels shame, guilt for murders," CNN, October 12, 2007, <http://edition.cnn.com/2007/US/10/09/soledad.DCsniper/index.html?iref=mpstoryview>, [accessed on July 19, 2015].

A Personal Experience

1. Matthew Rosenberg, "In Osama bin Laden Library: Illuminati and Bob Woodward," The New York Times, May 20, 2015, <http://www.nytimes.com/2015/05/21/world/asia/bin-laden-bookshelf-list-released-by-us-intelligence-agency.html?_r=0>, [accessed on July 19, 2015].

Chapter VII: Islam and Peace

Islam the Religion of Peace

1. Shuab al-Iman, al-Bayhaqi, 6006.

2. Al-Minhaj Sharh Sahih Muslim, Beirut, Dar Ihya al-Turath al-Arabi, 1972, Vol. 12, p. 229.

The Greatest Evil of History

1. Al-Trimidhi, Hadith no. 2202.
2. Sahih, Al-Bukhari, Book of the Holy War, Hadith no. 2957.
3. Sahih, Al-Bukhari, Hadith no. 121.

God Calls to the Home of Peace

1. Wahiduddin Khan, The Prophet of Peace, New Delhi, Penguin Books, 2009, p. 28.
2. Ismail ibn Kathir, Al-Bidayah wan Nihayah, Beirut, Dar Ihya al-Turath al-Arabi, 1988, Vol. 3, p. 327.
3. Musnad Ahmad, Hadith no. 7160.
4. Ismail ibn Kathir (author), Trevor Le Gassick [translator, The Life of the Prophet Muhammad, (Sirat ibn Kathir)], Berkshire, Garnet Publishing Limited, 1998, Vol. 2, p. 267.

Universal Peace Centre

1. Frederic Golden, "The Worst And The Brightest," Time, October 16, 2000.

Index

9/11, 109, 112

A

A New Theory of Evolution, 121

A Short History of Religions, 53

A.A. Khan, 156

Abbasid Caliphate, 89

Abbottabad, 157

Abel, 166

Abu Ala al-Afri, 31

Abu Bakr al-Baghdadi, 31, 98

Abu Dhabi, 120

Actual friends, 40

Adam and Eve, 41

Adolf Hitler, 76, 89

Afghanistan, 136

Africa, 126, 133, 142

Age of alternatives, 3, 30-31

Age of civilization, 3, 34-36

Age of peace, 3, 23, 26, 28, 115, 144, 173-174

Age of violence, 26

Ahsan al-qasas, 59

Ajniha al-Makar ath-Thalatha wa Khawafiha, 106

AK-47, 153

Aleppo, 89

Alexander the Great, 67, 76

Alfred Nobel, 175-176

Algiers, 133

Al-Imam al-Nawawi, 161

Allahabad, 156-157

Allied Powers, 20

Al-Urwah al Wuthqa (The Indissoluble Link), 136

America, 2, 80, 97, 112, 142, 146-147, 157

America's "War on Terrorism", 157

American expansionism, 106

Anachronism, 33, 116

Angel of Death, 157

Anger, 21, 34, 37, 80, 102-103, 121

Animal world, 48

Anti-Islam, 106

Anti-self activists, 149-150

Arabia, 53-54, 57, 60-61, 121

Arabs, 53, 71, 86, 121

Aristotle, 10

Armament industry, 111

Armed struggle, 33

Arms, 29, 90, 111, 153, 175-176

Arthur Keith, 121

Asculum, 76

Asia, 88-89, 133, 142,

Atom, 47-48, 80

Aurangzeb, 30

Azad Hind Fauj (Indian National Army), 56

B

Babylon, 67

Badr, 169

Balfour Declaration, 71, 86

Bangladesh, 80

Barack Obama, 98, 146

Battle of Hattin, 118

Battlefield, 28, 30, 78, 84, 91, 142, 170

Berlin Wall, 20

Bertrand Russell, 10

Bhawalpur Islamic University, 140

Bible, 40, 50, 59, 94,

Bilateral basis, 11

Bloodlines of the Illuminati by Fritz Springmeier, 158

Bob Woodward, 158

British East India Company, 101

British Empire, 77

British Mandate for Palestine, 86

British, 25, 53, 56, 77, 86, 89, 100-101, 121, 133

Buffer strategy, 63

C

Cain, 166

Caliphate, 89, 100, 121

Campaign, 80, 97, 103, 164

Character building, 171

Charles De Gaulle, 133-134

Children, 41, 122

China, 82-83

Christ, 39, 50-51

Christian Europe, 143, 145

Christian Mission, 106

Christian, 40, 106, 142-145, 153

Church, 40, 145, 153

Clear victory, 61

Colonialism, 106, 115, 133

Columbia University, 121

Companions of the Prophet, 6, 12, 54, 57, 60, 62, 109, 111, 156, 170

Common ancestry, 41

Communism, 68, 97, 106

Communist Empire, 68, 172

Confrontation, 11, 12, 36, 44, 53, 61, 62, 69, 75, 83, 84, 114, 122, 137, 161, 162, 169

Contribution of humanity, 37-39

Counter-ideology, 4, 93, 95, 182

Counter-violence, 56, 103

Country Threat Index (CTI), 70

Creation plan of God, 5, 24, 69, 116, 127, 129, 171-173

Creative community, 128

Creator, 3, 5-6, 24, 29, 44-45, 55, 74-75, 111, 117, 126-128, 131, 150-152, 163-164, 172-173

Crisis management, 3, 82-84

Culture of peace, 25, 91, 169, 177

D

Dar al-Insaan, 111

Dar al-Kufr (Land of Disbelief), 110

Dar as-Salam (Land of Islam), 110

Dara Shikoh, 30

David Cameron, 100

Dawah work, 32, 41, 132, 162

Dawah, 32, 41, 96, 114, 132, 162

Day of Resurrection, 29

De Gaulleism, 4, 133, 135

De-conditioning, 104

Democracy, 24, 26, 28, 32, 114, 162

De-monopolization, 3, 24-26

De-monopolize, 24

Deterrent factor, 155

Dichotomous thinking, 32

Difference management, 36

Disparities, 163

Disparity, 163-165

Divine rule, 95

Dr. Farida Khanam, 7

E

E.E. Kellet, 53

Eastern Europe, 97

Economic opportunities, 24, 26

Economist, 71

Edward Gibbon, 73

Egypt, 59-60, 82-83, 101, 121, 136, 139-140

Eighteenth century, 101-102

Elections, 26, 30

Encyclopaedia of Pacifism, 10

Enemies, 40, 71, 96, 102-103, 105, 117, 121, 130

Europe, 73, 88-89, 97, 126, 134, 142-143, 145

European, 73, 101, 115, 133, 143

F

Facebook, 107-108

Fajir, 27

Family, 39, 41-42

Fatwas, 110

Fiction, 123

First World War, 31, 48, 74

Formal education, 123

Forum for Promoting Peace in Muslim Societies, 120

Fourteenth century AD, 142

France, 82, 101, 133-134

Frederick Langbridge, 112

Freedom of thought, 126

Freedom, 13, 24-26, 45, 56, 80, 106-108, 114, 126-127, 133, 172

French North Africa, 133

French Revolution, 126, 172

G

Gabriel, 170

Gamal Abdel Nasser, 82, 86, 139

General Ayub Khan, 140

Geocentric Theory, 41

George Bush Jr., 76

Germany, 14, 20, 88-89

Ghazwa, 6, 62

Ghazwa al-Khandaq (The Battle of the Trench, 62

Global dissemination of the Quran, 120

Global distribution of the Quran, 120

God Almighty, 6, 24, 96, 128, 169

God, 4-7, 24, 27, 32, 41, 44, 46, 49, 53, 60, 69, 74-75, 94-96, 99, 103-104, 111, 113-114, 116, 120, 127-129, 132, 150-151, 162, 168-173, 176-177

Great Britain, 77

Greece, 67

Guerilla Air Defense: Antiaircraft Weapons and Techniques for Guerilla Forces by James Crabtree, 157

Gulf War, 147

Gun and bomb culture, 74, 104, 149

Guns and bombs, 29, 72, 98, 143, 155

H

Hadith, 57, 85, 132, 161-162, 167-168, 170

Harmony, 41, 47, 49

Hassan al-Banna, 86

Have-nots, 17, 25

Haves, 17, 25

Heaven, 110-111, 117

Heliocentric Theory, 41

Hell, 6, 109

Index

Heraclea, 76

High-profile, 136-137

Hijrah, 49

Hirohito, 88

Hiroshima, 80, 174

Historical laws, 87

Historical status quo, 3, 86

History, 3-4, 7, 10, 13, 16-17, 24-25, 27-29, 31, 37, 53, 55, 57-58, 65, 67-68, 73, 75-77, 79, 86-91, 94, 113, 118, 121, 137, 142-143, 145-148, 160, 166, 172-174

Holy See, 145

Home of Peace, 4, 49, 169, 171

Hong Kong, 82

Hudaybiyyah, 11, 57, 60, 171

Hudaybiyyah Agreement, 57, 60

Human life, 20, 36, 42, 91, 117, 123, 163-164

Human rights, 11-12, 105

Human society, 41, 66, 75, 139, 164

Human world, 20, 48-49, 139, 172

Humanity, 28, 34, 37-39, 42, 104, 137

Hyksos kings, 59

I

Ideal justice, 17-18, 66, 68

Idealism, 3, 14, 66, 181

Image of Islam, 134, 176-177

India, 2, 30, 56, 70, 77, 80-81, 101, 156

Indian army, 124

Indian subcontinent, 69

Individual peace, 13-14

Industrialization, 24

Informal education, 123

Injustice, 11-12, 16-18, 20, 74

Institutionalized buffer, 3, 62-63

Intellectual development, 36, 49

Intellectual freedom, 25

Intellectual revolution, 25, 28, 123, 126

Interdependence, 4, 163-165

International Labour Organization, 10, 18

Iran, 136

Iraq War, 76

Iraq, 63, 76, 98, 100, 145-146

Ishmaelite, 59

Islam, 4, 6, 11-12, 28, 44, 48-49, 89-90, 98-100, 102-106, 109-112, 120-121, 134, 140-141, 159-162, 167-168, 170, 176-177

Islamabad, 130

Islamic jihad, 166

Islamic scriptures, 164

Islamic State of Iraq and the Levant (ISIL), 100

Islamic terrorist movements, 98

Islamic texts, 99, 109

Islamic violence, 120

Islamophobia, 103, 107

Israelite, 59

Istishhad, 110

Italo-Turkish, 101, 116

Italy, 101, 145

Izvestia, 153

J

J.F. West, 25

Jamal ad-Din al-Afghani, 136

Jamia Hamdard, 7

Jamia Millia Islamia, 7

Japan, 14, 80, 88-89, 110

Jerusalem, 82, 86

Jesus Christ, 50-51

Jewish Supremacism, 94

Jews, 49, 94

Jihad, 40, 86, 95, 117, 166-167, 173

John Allen Muhammad, 154

Justice, 3, 10-12, 14, 16-19, 66, 68, 74, 99, 167

Justified war, 167

K

Kaaba, 53-54, 85-86

Kafir, 110

Kahlak, 156

Kashmir, 70, 124, 130

Khairuddin al-Zirikli, 117

Khalil Gibran, 109

Khazain al-Arz, 59

Khilafat, 100, 130

King Farouk, 82, 139

Kingdom of Italy, 101

Kingship, 31, 114, 139

Konrad Hermann Joseph Adenauer, 89

Kuwait, 63

L

Lateran Treaty, 145

Law of 'Repelling', 172

Law of nature, 4, 10-11, 14-16, 19, 21, 40-41, 44, 46, 48-49, 52, 54-55, 66-68, 71-72, 88, 131, 134-135, 137-138, 146-147, 163, 165

Lee Boyd Malvo, 154

Lee Kuan Yew, 70

Literary bomb, 4, 97-98

Literary campaign, 97

Lord Mountbatten, 77

Low profile, 4, 52, 136

M

Mad'u, 96

Madinah Declaration, 49

Madinah, 49, 51, 62, 111

Mahatma Gandhi, 10, 56

Major Akbar Khan, 170

Makkah, 49, 51-54, 60, 62, 85

Malaysia, 70

Maria Khan, 7

Martyr, 110

Martyrdom, 110

Mashhud, 96

Mass education, 124

Max Hospital, 5

Means of communication, 28, 120, 127

Media, 32, 74, 98, 101-103, 105-108, 120, 123, 174, 176

Mediterranean Sea, 101

Messenger, 6

Michael H. Hart, 57

Michel Chossudovsky, 157

Mikhail Kalashnikov, 153

Militancy, 91, 95, 99, 101-102, 124, 127, 134, 139

Milovan Djilas, 97

Modern age, 25-26, 29-30, 75, 103-104, 115-116, 118, 127, 141, 144

Modern civilization, 24-25, 28, 35, 42, 63, 73, 113

Modern education, 64, 104, 141

Modern technology, 37, 63, 78, 113, 115, 120

Monarchy, 28, 172

Mongol, 89

Monotheism, 53, 60, 160

Mosul, 98

Mughal, 30, 101

Muhammad Abduh, 136

Muhammad Ali Jinnah, 69

Mujahid, 118

Mujahideen, 167

Muslim community, 102-103, 105, 109-110, 116, 128, 130, 132, 134, 141, 166, 177

Muslim leaders, 134-135, 141, 146, 148

Muslim media, 101-103

Muslim militancy, 95, 101-102, 134, 139

Muslim supremacism, 94

Muslim world, 4, 32, 101-102, 111, 125, 128, 139

Muslim youth, 103-104, 120, 136

Muslimophobia, 104

Muslims, 4, 32, 49, 85-86, 89-90, 94, 96, 99, 101-104, 106-113, 115-118, 120-121, 128, 130-132, 134-135, 139, 141-145, 166-169, 171, 176-177

Mutual consultation, 160

N

Nagasaki, 80, 174

Napoleon Bonaparte, 101

Nation building, 21

Negative thinking, 81, 88, 90, 102, 108

New Delhi, 5, 7, 112, 158

New York, 109, 112-113

Nineteenth centuries, 143

Nobel Prize, 175

Non-confrontational, 3, 43-44, 69

Non-interference, 3, 20, 47-49

Non-political empire, 32

Non-political fields, 32, 61, 147

Non-political message, 170

Non-self activists, 150-151

Non-state actors, 70, 167, 173

Normalcy, 11-14, 16-17, 20, 60, 84

Nuclear bomb, 97

Nuclear Disarmament Forum, 112

O

Obama's Wars, 158

Okinawa, 14

Opportunities, 11-12, 16, 18-19, 24-26, 48, 50-52, 54-55, 57, 61, 75, 78, 86, 114-115, 140-141, 152

Oppression, 68, 167

Orientalism, 106

Osama bin Laden, 98, 157

Ottoman Empire, 31, 86, 101

Ottoman Navy, 101

Outdated mindset, 26, 115

P

Pacifism, 3, 10

Pacifist, 156

Pakistan, 69-71, 80-81, 130, 140-141

Pakistani, 69-70, 80, 95, 130

Palestine, 71, 83, 86, 96, 130

Paradise, 49, 77, 160, 167, 169

Paris, 136

Partition after Partition, 80

Partition Plan for Palestine, 86

Partition, 69-70, 80, 86, 130

Patience, 58, 63, 83-84

Patriarch Kirill, 153

Peace at any cost, 14, 19

Peace bomb, 155

Peace for the sake of normalcy, 12

Peace for the sake of social justice, 12

Peace of mind, 4, 13, 126

Peace on a unilateral basis, 16

Peace Research Institute (SIPRI), 174

Peace through education, 4, 122, 124

Peaceful alternative, 120

Peaceful atmosphere, 12, 71, 127

Peaceful crusades, 143

Peaceful dialogue, 36, 63

Peaceful method, 21, 29, 31, 41, 44, 51, 58, 60, 68, 72, 75, 90, 134, 137

Peaceful negotiations, 36, 82

Peaceful planning, 3, 15, 58, 69, 71, 77, 89-90, 141

Peaceful society, 123

Peaceful strategy, 52, 56-57, 83, 143

Peaceful struggle, 78, 95, 147, 152, 157

Peace-loving, 121, 156, 169

Pearl Harbour, 80

Pervez Musharraf, 70

Philadelphia, 40

Philip K Hitti, 90

Planets, 47

Policy of delinking, 3, 53-55

Political activism, 11, 32, 87, 147

Political adjustment, 59

Political authority, 60, 147

Political empires, 32

Political Islam, 100

Political leader, 136

Political power, 24-26, 99, 114-115, 131, 146-147, 160-161, 164

Political status quo, 59

Pope, 145

Positive alternative, 121

Positive bomb, 121

Positive thinking, 50, 81, 90, 104

Potential friends, 40

Pragmatism, 3, 14, 66-67

Present-day Muslims, 4, 32, 94, 101, 116

Printing press, 28, 101, 105, 107, 124

Priyanka Chopra, 149

Progress and development, 55, 70, 90, 133

Progress, 13, 49, 55, 70, 90, 115, 117, 128, 133-134

Prophet Abraham, 53, 85

Prophet Joseph, 59-61, 140

Prophet Muhammad, 51-54, 57-58, 60-62, 85, 111, 169

Prophet of Islam, 6, 11, 44, 49, 111, 120, 168

Pro-self activists, 150-151

Pyrrhic victory, 76

Pyrrhic War, 76

Pyrrhus of Epirus, 76

Q

Qital, 161, 167

Quran, 5, 27, 29, 40, 42, 47, 49, 52, 59, 61, 69, 91, 94, 96, 99, 101, 103, 113-114, 119-121, 128, 131-132, 160-163, 167-169, 171-172

Quranic, 40, 59, 99, 121, 132, 160, 163, 173

Quzman, 6

R

Radicalization, 4, 101-103

Raheel Sharif, 130

Reader's Digest, 97

Realistic planning, 55

Re-engineering of the mind, 123

Reformers, 13, 17, 32, 66, 104-105, 162

Religion of peace, 4, 160, 162, 177

Religion, 4, 24, 27-28, 49, 74, 90, 104, 106, 134, 160, 162, 174, 176-177

Religious freedom, 114

Religious persecution, 114

Renaissance, 143

Revolution, 7, 25, 28-29, 123, 126, 140, 172

Robert Hopkins Miller, 158

Roman Empire, 73, 126

Romans, 27, 76

Rome, 145

Russo-Turkish War, 101

S

Saddam Hussein, 31, 98, 145-148

Sahih al-Bukhari, 85, 109

Salahuddin Ayyubi, 118

Salahuddin, 118

Sassanid Persia, 27

Sayyid Abul Ala Maududi, 95, 140

Sayyid Qutb, 86, 95, 118, 139-140

Science and technology, 32, 118

Science, 25, 27, 32, 36, 118, 134

Scientific age, 143

Second Millennium BC, 85

Second World War, 14, 20, 48, 68, 74, 77, 79, 88, 110, 174

Secret of success, 51-52, 58, 138

Seed, 20, 45, 138

Self-styled, 5, 68, 95, 100, 127, 173

Semitic, 59

Seyyed Vali Reza Nasr, 140

Shahid, 96

Shariah, 130

Shaykh Abd ar-Rahman Hasan Habannaka al-Maydani, 105

Sheikh Mujibur Rahman, 80

Sinai Peninsula, 82

Singapore, 70-71

Six-Day War, 82

Social justice, 10-12, 14, 17-18

Social media, 103, 107

Social peace, 13-14, 39, 165

Soviet Russia, 68

Soviet Union, 97

Spiritual Crusades, 142

St. Augustine, 10

Stars, 47, 112

Status quo, 3, 14-15, 18, 59, 85-87, 164-165

Status quoism, 14, 164

Stockholm, Sweden, 175

Stone Age, 34, 37

Subhas Chandra Bose, 56

Suez Canal Company, 82

Suez Canal, 82

Suez Crisis, 82

Suicide bombings, 6, 95, 101-103, 109-111, 168

Summum bonum, 3, 13, 15

Sunnah, 86, 101, 103

Sword, 78, 109, 121, 166

Syria, 100

Syrian, 83, 105, 117

T

T.W. Arnold, 89

Tahera Ahmad, 107

Tartar, 89

Tawhid, 60, 160

Technology, 28, 32, 34, 36-37, 63, 78, 113, 115, 118, 120

Terrorism, 4, 78, 95, 98-100, 105, 120-121, 128, 150, 153-155, 157-158, 173

Terrorist, 4, 46, 78, 98, 100, 119, 121, 127, 154-155, 173

The best story, 59-60

The Book That Is Shaking the Communist World, 97

The Book That Is Shaking the Terrorist World, 98

The Crusades, 4, 142-144

The Dismemberment of Pakistan, 80

The life Hereafter, 151

The message of God, 32, 41, 95-96, 114, 162

The New Class: An Analysis of the Communist System, 97

The Preaching of Islam, 89

Thirteenth century, 89

Tradition, 6, 27, 44, 109, 120, 170

Translations of the Quran, 119

Tree, 15, 20, 45, 75, 77, 96, 109, 128, 138, 148, 150, 156

Trendsetter, 4, 69, 142, 144

Tripoli, 116

Tripolitania, 101

Turkey, 31-32, 136

Twelfth century, 118

Twentieth century, 77-78, 89, 113

Twenty-first century, 29, 31, 63, 78, 144, 148, 168

Twin Towers, 109, 113

U

U.S., 158

UN Charter, 63

Ulama, 110, 161

Umm al-Ma'arik (Mother of All Battles), 147

Ummah, 166, 168

Unilateral basis, 11-12, 16

Unilateralism, 11

Un-Islamic, 99, 167

United Kingdom, 82

Universal Peace Centre, 4, 175-177

Universe, 1, 27, 47, 49, 91, 113, 128, 139, 150

Unlawful, 109-111, 161

Unrealistic goal, 147

USSR, 68, 97

V

V.P. Fortna, 121

Vegetarian, 156

Vietnam 84, 158

Vatican City, 145

Vietnam War, 84

Violent bomb, 121, 155

W

War, 5, 6, 10-12, 14, 19-26, 29-35, 37, 40-42, 48, 57, 60, 62-63, 68, 70, 73-84, 87-90, 96, 100-101, 110, 115-116, 118, 122, 124, 131, 142-144, 148, 157-158, 160-162, 166-168, 170-171, 174

War and violence, 25, 29, 33, 35, 75, 77, 81, 83, 90, 162

War culture, 24-25

Washington Metropolitan Area, 154

Washington, 154

Weapons, 33, 77, 121, 128, 153, 157, 168, 174, 176

West, 3, 20, 25, 27, 103-104, 108

West Germany, 20

Western civilization, 3, 27-28, 143

Western nations, 27, 143-144

White House, 146

Wisdom of children, 122

Wise planning, 11-12, 15-16, 19, 50, 57, 60-61, 63-64, 83, 141

Witnesses of God, 94

Working justice, 17-18

World Hereafter, 6, 151, 160

World Trade Centre (WTC), 109

Y

Yasser Arafat, 118

Yugoslavia, 97

Z

Zionism, 106

Zug, Switzerland, 112